THE CASE AGAINST
SCHOOL
VOUCHERS

The Authors

Edd Doerr, executive director of Americans for Religious Liberty since 1982, is a former teacher in public and private schools and is the author or co-author of fifteen books.

Albert J. Menendez, associate director and research director of Americans for Religious Liberty, is a former public school teacher and author or co-author of thirty books.

The Rev. John M. Swomley (Ph.D., political science; M.A.; S.T.B.), president of Americans for Religious Liberty, is Professor Emeritus of Christian Ethics at the St. Paul School of Theology in Kansas City, Missouri, a United Methodist institution, and the author of eight books.

R

THE CASE AGAINST
SCHOOL
VOUCHERS

**Edd Doerr
Albert J. Menendez
John M. Swomley**

Prometheus Books

59 John Glenn Drive
Amherst, NewYork 14228-2197

in cooperation with
Americans for Religious Liberty
P.O. Box 6656
Silver Springs, Maryland 20916

Published 1996 by Prometheus Books
in cooperation with Americans for Religious Liberty

00 99 98 97 96   5 4 3 2 1

Library of Congress Cataloging-in-Publication Data

Doerr, Edd.
    The case against school vouchers / Edd Doerr, Albert J.
Menendez, John M. Swomley.
        p.   cm.
    Includes bibliographical references (p.   ).
    ISBN 1–57392–092–4 (pbk. : alk. paper)
    1. Educational vouchers—United States. 2. School
choice—United States. I. Menendez, Albert J. II. Swomley,
John M., 1915–   . III. Title.
LB2828.8.D64   1996
379.1'1—dc20   96–24370
                                                        CIP

Printed in the United States of America on acid-free paper.

For Herenia, Shirley, and Marjie

Contents

Acknowledgments

We wish to express our appreciation for the inestimable skills of our colleague Marie Gore. Without her assistance neither this book nor much of our other work would get done. We also appreciate the work on which we have drawn by many individuals and organizations too numerous to list.

Introduction and Summary

Should public funds be used to support nonpublic education? Controversy over that question has raged since early in the nineteenth century. In recent years it has involved Congress and state legislatures, federal and state courts, twenty state referenda, battles fought in scholarly journals and the popular press, the intrusion of religion into politics, and partisan political warfare.

In the 1990s the debate centers around elementary and secondary school tuition vouchers, sometimes called "scholarships" or, as in a plan included in mid-1995 in Ohio Gov. George Voinovich's budget to circumvent the normal legislative process, "tutorial assistance grants." Variants of the voucher idea include tuition reimbursement through federal or state tax credits. Many different voucher plans have been proposed with varying levels of per-student aid, but what they all have in common is payment from public funds for expenses incurred for nonpublic education.

The case for vouchers can be presented rather simply. Voucher advocates claim that failure to include nonpublic schooling in public funding for elementary and secondary education is unfair, that vouchers will promote diversity in education, and that school "choice" plans involving nonpublic schools will improve the quality and effectiveness of education.

The authors, who have spent an aggregate total of more than eighty-five years researching and writing about this controversy, believe not only that the case for tuition vouchers is extremely weak but also that the case against vouchers is overwhelmingly strong.

It is the plan of this book to summarize the case against vouchers succinctly in this introduction and then provide evidence and documentation for each argument.

We hope that this concise treatment of the tuition voucher issue will help lawmakers, opinion leaders, and ordinary citizens understand that voucher proposals pose serious threats to religious freedom, to our stressed economy, to our great system of democratic common schools, to community and interfaith harmony, and to other core American values.

The elements of the argument against vouchers need not be read in any order. Each one may be regarded as dispositive, while all together they constitute a solid and irrefutable case.

Summary of the Case against Tuition Vouchers

1. Vouchers threaten the religious liberty of every American because they would compel all taxpayers to contribute involuntarily to the support of religious institutions. The overwhelming majority of nonpublic elementary and secondary students attend pervasively sectarian or denominational institutions.

2. Vouchers would seriously dilute voter and taxpayer control over public spending. Unlike our country's 15,500 public school districts, nonpublic schools are not and would not be under meaningful public control by popularly elected authorities. Vouchers are "taxation without representation."

3. Vouchers violate the letter and the spirit of the U.S. and state constitutions.

4. Most Americans oppose vouchers, as both state referenda and opinion polls have clearly shown.

5. Vouchers would provide public subsidies for schools that commonly select and/or attract students and teachers along lines related to religion, ideology, ethnicity, academic ability level, handicaps, etc., forms of selectivity not allowed in public schools. A high degree of sectarian self-selectivity results from the very nature of most nonpublic schools, from the content of their textbooks, and from the religion or ideology that generally pervades nonpublic school curricula.

6. The forms of selectivity and discrimination common in nonpublic schools would lead in turn to the balkanization or fragmentation of our children, communities, and society along religious, ideological, ethnic, social class, and other lines.

7. Vouchers would increase school costs while lowering educational quality. Vouchers would lead to higher taxes or cutbacks in funding for public schools or both.

8. Vouchers would tend to aid the well-off disproportionately while leaving the poor, the handicapped, and minorities worse off.

9. Vouchers would inevitably weaken and possibly even wreck public education, a mainstay of American democracy. Vouchers would tend to turn public schools into institutions of last resort for the poor, the handicapped, and minorities.

10. Vouchers in the long run would result in shifting teachers into posts where they would likely be tested for religious or ideological orthodoxy. This would mean a loss of academic freedom for teachers and a loss to students of the diversity and pluralism found in public schools.

11. Vouchers would tend to favor religious bodies large enough to assemble enough students to operate a viable school, and to discriminate against smaller religious bodies and against people of those religious persuasions that oppose separating children by creed.

12. Vouchers could in the long run lead to a level of public regulation that nonpublic school sponsors would

find burdensome to their religious mission. Further, growing dependence on government support would likely cause the atrophy of nonpublic schools' ability to raise money privately should they choose for whatever reason to give up public funding.

13. A voucher plan regulated to eliminate all forms of discrimination would require a large, costly, and cumbersome public bureaucracy.

14. Voucher advocates' claims that voucher or extensive school choice plans would reduce educational costs and improve educational performance are unfounded.

15. Voucher plans could present a cruel choice to religious groups that operate private schools but do not want to accept public funding, whether out of religious principle, to avoid becoming dependent on government largesse, or to remain free of burdensome government regulations that might reasonably be expected to follow public funding.

16. The idea that "competition" with nonpublic schools will somehow improve public schools lacks empirical support.

17. The primary beneficiaries of a voucher plan will be the nearly five million students already attending nonpublic schools and the religious bodies that sponsor those schools.

18. While voucher promoters often complain that people who pay taxes for public schools and also tuition for nonpublic schools are "double taxed," the truth is that they are taxed but once, for the public schools are

open to, serve, and are governed by all the people. A voucher plan would truly be a "double taxation"; citizens would be taxed once for the support of public schools, and again and again and again for all the different non-public schools receiving tax support.

19. Vouchers would move tax-funded American education away from the present system of democratic control, pluralism, and accountability toward a maze of multiple school systems often typified by selectivity, discrimination, and a closed intellectual world not responsible to or accountable to the taxpaying public.

20. If voucher legislation is enacted and somehow survives a court test, the damage to our country would be irreversible.

The authors do not question the right of religious bodies to operate private schools or the right of parents to send their children to them. What we object to is government support of religious institutions which are integral parts of a religious body's religious mission, government support for the kinds of selectivity common in nonpublic schools, and the use of the taxing power of government to compel involuntary support for religious institutions.

1

Vouchers Would Undermine Religious Liberty

The overwhelming majority of nonpublic schools that would receive public funding under a voucher plan are religious institutions. They are frequently described by their supporters as integral parts of the sponsoring religious body's mission, ministry, or apostolate. It follows that vouchers would undermine that most precious of our liberties, religious liberty.

This point was made most eloquently by James Madison, chief architect of both the Constitution and the Bill of Rights, in his justly famous 1785 Memorial and Remonstrance Against Religious Assessments. Madison wrote:

> It is proper to take alarm at the first experiment on our liberties. . . .
> Who does not see . . . that the same authority which

can force a citizen to contribute three pence only of his property for the support of any one establishment, may force him to conform to any other establishment in all cases whatsoever. . . .

The Bill [Patrick Henry's bill to provide tax support for the teaching of religion] implies either that the Civil Magistrate is a competent Judge of Religious Truth; or that he may employ Religion as an engine of Civil policy. The first is an arrogant pretention falsified by the contradictory opinions of Rulers in all ages, and throughout the world; the second is an unhallowed perversion of the means of salvation. . . .

Madison's Memorial led to the defeat of Henry's bill to provide nonpreferential aid to all religions, which bore a certain resemblance to today's voucher proposals, and to the subsequent passage of Jefferson's Bill for Establishing Religious Freedom (1785), which declares, in part:

That to compel a man to furnish contributions of money for the propagation of opinions which he disbelieves and abhors, is sinful and tyrannical; that even the forcing him to support this or that teacher of his own religious persuasion, is depriving him of the comfortable liberty of giving his contributions to the particular pastor whose morals he would make his pattern. . . .

We, the General Assembly of Virginia, do enact that no man shall be compelled to frequent or support any religious worship, place, or ministry whatsoever, nor shall be enforced, restrained, molested, or burthened in his body or goods, or shall otherwise suffer, on account of his religious opinions or belief; but that all men shall be free to profess, and by argument to maintain, their opinions in matters of religion, and that the same shall in no wise diminish, enlarge, or affect their civil capacities.

The operative language of the Bill is today part of the Virginia Bill of Rights, and that language or its spirit is found today in most state constitutions.

This Jeffersonian-Madisonian principle—no laws respecting an establishment of religion, no taxes for religious purposes, separation of church and state—is implied in the United States Constitution of 1787 and made more explicit in the First Amendment (1789). Indeed, the separation principle was so universally approved that it was incorporated into the Constitution of the Confederate States of America in 1861.

The tie between the general American devotion to religious liberty and longstanding public opposition to tax aid for denominational schools is so strong that merely listing all the religious leaders, statesmen, scholars, and editorial writers who have endorsed the principle of religious freedom and no tax for religion would be exhausting.

The most recent major expression of support for that principle is the statement "A Shared Vision; Religious Liberty in the 21st Century," endorsed by a long list of Christian and Jewish leaders and organizations and formally presented to Vice President Al Gore in July of 1994. That statement declares, in part:

We agree with Jefferson and Madison that it is wrong to tax citizens to support the teaching of religion. In the words of the Virginia Statute for Establishing Religious Freedom: "No man shall be compelled to frequent or support any religious worship, place, or ministry whatsoever. . . ." Therefore, we oppose direct or indirect government funding of parochial schools at primary and secondary levels and of pervasively sectarian colleges and universities. . . .

Our heritage of religious liberty and church-state separation must be reaffirmed. The increasing religious pluralism in our country beckons us to turn this heritage into a legacy. The aspirations of the Founders—that religion should involve a voluntary response and that government should remain neutral toward religion—must be converted into practical reality. Daniel Carroll of Maryland said it well over 200 years ago when he declared that "the rights of conscience are . . . of particular delicacy and will little bear the gentlest touch of governmental hand." Carroll's lofty view of conscience captures our understanding of our past and guides our vision of the future. We commit ourselves to making this ideal a reality as we approach the 21st Century.[1]

Further support for the principle that religious liberty requires church-state separation and the confining of tax support to public schools is found in the National Committee for Public Education and Religious Liberty (PEARL), a national coalition of national, regional, and local religious, parents', educators', and civic organizations founded in 1972. PEARL has supported litigation in the Supreme Court and lower courts in defense of that principle.[2]

The fact that a number of other countries (Canada,

the United Kingdom, France, Belgium, Australia, the Netherlands, Ireland, etc.) tax their citizens for the support of sectarian schools is often cited by voucher advocates as a reason for the United States to do likewise. But these residues of Old World religious establishments have created bitter social and political divisions along religious lines of the kind that we Americans have largely had the wisdom and foresight to avoid by inventing and implementing the constitutional principle of separation of church and state. For the United States to emulate the mistakes of other countries would be to forget the lessons of history, to reject the separation arrangement that has given our country a higher degree of religious freedom than any society has ever known, to retrogress to the kind of society that drove many of our ancestors to these shores in the first place.

Religious liberty is our most precious heritage. Vouchers for nonpublic schools would sabotage that heritage.

United Methodist minister and seminary professor John M. Swomley has summarized the reasons why religious bodies and persons should support the principle of church-state separation and no taxes for religion:

1. Church-state separation prevents government from determining church policy, whether directly or indirectly.

2. Separation does not permit churches to seek special privileges from government that are denied to minority religious groups and to religiously unaffiliated persons.

3. Churches are healthier and stronger if they assume responsibility both for financing their own programs and

for stimulating their members to accept that responsibility.

4. By operating independently of government aid, the churches deny to government the power to impose compulsory tithes on all taxpayers, believers and nonbelievers alike. The churches thus avoid the resentment of those who do not want to be forced to contribute to churches to which they do not belong and of their own members who do not welcome being forced to contribute through government action.

5. Since separation precludes financial support or special privilege from government, the churches are free to engage in prophetic criticism of the government and to work for social justice.

6. The mission of the churches is compromised by government aid to church schools that serve chiefly middle- and upper-class students. Church empires are costly and require additional private funds from those who use the services, thus tending to exclude millions of poor people.

7. Government sponsorship of religious activity, including prayer services, sacred symbols, religious festivals, and the like, tends to secularize the religious activity rather than make government more ethical or religious.

8. The churches' witness in other nations is greater if they are not identified with or dependent upon specific governments. The Reformed Church was identified with the old all-white government of South Africa and its apartheid policy. The Roman Catholic Church was closely

identified with the Franco and Salazar dictatorships in Spain and Portugal.[3]

More recently, it might be noted, the Serbian Orthodox Church has come to be identified with the policies of Serbia (Yugoslavia).

Another important point that needs to be made in the voucher debate is that tax-paid vouchers would thrust government into the middle of an intra-church controversy. Among Catholics, for instance, there has been since the mid-nineteenth century a division over whether Catholics should have separate schools or send their children to public schools. Widespread anti-Catholic bias, added to official church teaching, led to the development of a system of Catholic parochial schools that at its high point enrolled about half of all Catholic students. But the fading of anti-Catholic feeling since World War II and the increasing respect for religious pluralism in public schools has led to a sharp drop in parochial school enrollment from 5.5 million in 1965 to about half that figure in 1995. Increasing numbers of Catholics, now about three-fourths, place their children in public schools and do not wish to support parochial schools, whether through voluntary tuition or taxes. As a Catholic member of the Wisconsin legislature told one of the authors several years ago, "We voted in our parish not to have a parish school and we certainly do not want the state to make us pay taxes to support them." A voucher plan, then, would intrude government into an intra-church controversy and tax Catholics for private schools most today choose not to patronize or support.

Finally, just as the United States pioneered the arrangements we label federalism, separation of powers, and checks and balances as means to try to prevent excessive concentrations of power and strengthen individual freedom, so too does our church-state separation arrangement work to prevent the joining together of government and ecclesiastical power, which history has abundantly shown to be inimical to personal, intellectual, and religious liberty.

Notes

1. Signers of the "Shared Vision" statement include: Al Albergate, The Rev. Dr. Jimmy R. Allen, Mimi Alperin, American Jewish Committee, American Jewish Congress, Americans for Religious Liberty, Dr. Nancy T. Ammerman, Dr. Sarah Frances Anders, Baptist Joint Committee, General Board of Baptist State Convention of North Carolina, John F. Baugh, Dr. B. Bert Beach, The Rev. Dr. John Leland Berg, The Rev. Charles Bergstrom, Rabbi Louis Bernstein, The Rev. John Buchanan, Scott Bunton, The Rev. John Burns, The Rev. Dr. Joan Brown Campbell, Jerome Chanes, Dr. Harvey Cox, The Rev. Dr. Calvin Didier, Edd Doerr, Bishop R. Sheldon Duecker, The Rev. Dr. James M. Dunn, The Rev. Dr. William R. Estep, The Rev. David Albert Farmer, The Rev. Dr. Ronald B. Flowers, Richard T. Foltin, Steven M. Freeman, Bishop Edwin R. Garrison, Dr. Edwin S. Gaustad, Dr. Alan Geyer, The Rev. Elenora Giddings Ivory, Rabbi Joseph B. Glaser, Rabbi Alfred Gottschalk, Rabbi Leonard Guttman, James A. Hamilton, Dr. Robert T. Handy, The Rev. Dr. Stan Hastey, The Rev. Dr. E. Glenn Hinson, The Rev. Dr. Clint Hopkins, Dr. Gregg Ivers, The Rev. Dr. Dan Ivins, Norman Jameson, The Rev. R. Mark Jordan, The Rev. Dean M. Kelley, The Rev. Dr. Thomas Kilgore,

Jr., John Klingenstein, Norman Lear, The Rev. Dr. Bill J. Leonard, Charles Levendosky, The Rev. Dr. Dean H. Lewis, Rabbi Mordechai Liebling, Robert Lipshutz, The Rev. Barry Lynn, The Rev. Dr. Robert L. Maddox, The Rev. Dr. Dean Majette, Rabbi Joel H. Meyers, Alfred H. Moses, The Rev. Dr. James A. Nash, National Council of Churches of Christ in the U.S.A., The Rev. Dr. Alan Neely, People for the American Way, The Rev. Troy W. Petty, Dr. Richard Pierard, Samuel Rabinove, The Rev. Dr. Robert Rainwater, The Rev. J. George Reed, The Rev. Dr. John E. Roberts, Dr. Gary M. Ross, Rabbi A. James Rudin, Rabbi David Saperstein, The Rev. Dr. David Sapp, Rabbi Alexander Schindler, The Rev. Dr. Cecil Sherman, Donald W. Shriver, Jr., Peggy L. Shriver, Carroll D. Stevens, Rabbi Alan Silverstein, The Rev. Dr. Wallace Charles Smith, Marc D. Stern, Phil D. Strickland, The Rev. Dr. John Swomley, Rabbi David A. Teutsch, The Rev. Oliver S. Thomas, The Rev. Robert W. Tiller, Earl Trent, The Rev. Tim Turnham, The Rev. J. Brent Walker, The Rev. Bill Wilson, The Rev. Dr. Phillip Wogaman, The Rev. Aidsand Wright-Riggins.

2. The organizations in the National Coalition for Public and Religious Liberty include: American Association of School Administrators; American Association of University Women; American Civil Liberties Union; American Ethical Union; American Federation of Teachers; American Humanist Association; American Jewish Congress; Americans for Democratic Action, New York City Chapter; Americans for Religious Liberty; Americans United for Separation of Church and State (and Rochester, New York, Chapter); Anti-Defamation League; A. Philip Randolph Institute; Arizona Citizens Project; Association of Reform Rabbis of New York City and Vicinity; Baptist Joint Committee; Central Conference of American Rabbis; City Club of New York; Community Church of New York, Social Action Committee; Council of Churches of the City of New York; Council for Democratic and Secular Humanism; Council

of Supervisors and Administrators; Episcopal Diocese of Long Island, Committee on Social Concerns and Peace; Episcopal Diocese of New York; Federation of Reconstructionist Congregations and Havurot; Freedom to Learn Network; Freethought Society of Greater Philadelphia; Hadassah; Humanist Society of Metropolitan New York; Institute for First Amendment Studies; League for Industrial Democracy, New York City Chapter; Michigan Council About Parochiaid; Minnesota Civil Liberties Union; Monroe County, New York, PEARL; National Council of Jewish Women; National Center for Science Education; National Education Association; National Emergency Civil Liberties Committee; National PTA; New York Jewish Labor Committee; New York Society for Ethical Culture; New York State Congress of Parents and Teachers; New York State Council of Churches; New York State School Boards Association; New York State United Teachers; Ohio PEARL; Parents' Coalition for Education in New York City; Public Education Association; Union of American Hebrew Congregations; New York Federation of Reform Synagogues; Unitarian Universalist Association; United Church of Christ; United Community Centers; United Federation of Teachers; United Synagogues of America, New York Metropolitan Region; Washington Area Secular Humanists; Women's American O.R.T.; Women's City Club of New York; Workmen's Circle, New York Division.

   3. John M. Swomley, *Religious Liberty and the Secular State* (Amherst, N.Y.: Prometheus Books, 1987), pp. 14–15.

2

Vouchers: The People Say No

The American people do not favor tax support for parochial or private schools. They have said so repeatedly, where it matters, in the polling booths of the nation. This issue has been placed before the electorate twenty times since 1966, and the voters rejected it nineteen times. Voters in thirteen states and the District of Columbia have considered variants of the voucher/tax credit schemes and, with the single exception of South Dakota, they have rejected all of them.

In these twenty elections, 62.6 percent of voters have rejected various and sundry proposals to divert tax funds to church-related schools. If the states were weighted by population, the average negative vote rises to 66.9 percent, or two out of three voters. The most recent Gallup survey, released on August 22, 1995, found that, nation-

27

wide, Americans oppose vouchers 65 percent to 33 percent. (See below.) It is essential to note, also, that one-third of all Americans live in states where the people have already cast a direct yes or no vote on parochiaid, and, as we have seen, a solid majority have said no. (See Table 1.)

The most common type of parochiaid measure was the proposal to weaken the state constitutions to allow subsequent legislatures to pass various aid proposals. Constitutional changes were rejected by voters in New York (1967), Oregon (1972), Washington State (1975), Alaska (1976), and Massachusetts (1986). Auxiliary services, often including textbooks, transportation, and other incidentals, were turned down by voters in Maryland (1974), Missouri (1976), and Massachusetts (1982). Vouchers were rejected in Maryland (1972), Michigan (1978), Colorado (1992), and California (1993). Bus transportation was rejected by voters in Nebraska (1966) and Idaho (1972). Voters in the District of Columbia (1981) and Oregon (1990) turned down tuition tax credits, the equivalent of vouchers. Tuition reimbursement for parochial schools was rejected by Nebraska voters in 1970. Textbooks were rejected by California voters in 1982 but approved in South Dakota in 1986.

In Michigan in 1970 voters opposed to constant attempted raids on the state treasury by private and parochial school lobbies initiated and approved an amendment to the state constitution banning all forms of tax aid to nonpublic education.

Advocates of tax aid or support for sectarian and other nonpublic schools often claim wide support for their point of view. Their claims, however, are usually based on poorly designed poll questions. While permit-

Table 1

STATE REFERENDA ON PAROCHIAID, 1966–1993

YEAR	STATE	% AGAINST	%FOR
1966	Nebraska	57%	43%
1967	New York	72%	27%
1970	Nebraska	57%	43%
1970	Michigan	57%	43%
1972	Oregon	61%	39%
1972	Idaho	57%	43%
1972	Maryland	55%	45%
1974	Maryland	56%	43%
1975	Washington	60%	39%
1976	Alaska	54%	46%
1976	Missouri	60%	40%
1978	Michigan	74%	26%
1981	District of Columbia	89%	11%
1982	California	61%	39%
1982	Massachusetts	62%	38%
1986	Massachusetts	70%	30%
1986	South Dakota	46%	54%
1990	Oregon	67%	33%
1992	Colorado	67%	33%
1993	California	70%	30%

ting families greater choice among public schools is at least a superficially popular idea, mixing together public school choice and tax support for nonpublic schools in a single poll question to be answered "yes" or "no" is sure to produce ambiguous if not meaningless results.

However, when the issue is placed concretely before a

large group of voters, with advocates and opponents of the proposed constitutional amendment or law slugging it out in the public arena and the media, then a meaningful test of public opinion is possible. As we have seen, electorates educated about the parochiaid issue in a rough and tumble election campaign almost invariably (94 percent of the time in the last quarter century) vote no on diverting public funds to nonpublic schools, even though the opponents of aid are almost always outspent by a considerable margin.

Other valid tests of public opinion occurred in the 1970s when the Nixon and Ford administrations put considerable effort and money into trying to get individual school districts to experiment with federally funded voucher schemes. Despite all that effort, only one district in the nation, the Alum Rock district in San Jose, California, agreed to participate in a three-year experiment, and only after stipulating that no religious schools whatever be involved. The experiment was not considered a success. Efforts by the Ford administration to sell a federally funded voucher plan to communities in New Hampshire and Connecticut came to naught when local opinion polls, sponsored by the voucher promoters, consistently rejected the plans.

Promoting vouchers, then, would seem to be the wrong horse for a politician to hitch a wagon to, though some politicians in some areas might gain from it. Parochiaid supporters are more likely to be single-issue voters than parochiaid opponents.

Unfortunately, the parochiaiders' horrendous losing streak is not widely known. For obscure reasons about which we can only speculate, the media have largely ignored this quarter century of electoral defeats for parochiaid. They rarely rate a mention outside the states in which they occur, and generally receive far less coverage than referenda on far less significant matters.

While referenda over a quarter of a century, involving an aggregate total of millions of voters and following intensive political and media campaigns, have shown clearly that most Americans oppose vouchers, opinion polls have been a bit less clear, due often to the use of confusing or ambiguous questions by pollsters.

Probably the most well known polls relating to vouchers are those done by the Gallup organization and Phi Delta Kappa (PDK), the educators fraternity, eight times between 1970 and 1991. These polls have been interpreted by some as favoring vouchers, since "approval" over the twenty-one-year span ranged from 38 percent to 51 percent and averaged 45 percent, while "disapproval" ranged 38 percent to 46 percent and averaged 41.25 percent.[1]

The problem, however, lay with the nature of the poll question used: "In some nations, the government allows a certain amount of money for each child's education. The parents can then send the child to any public, parochial, or private school they choose. This is called the 'voucher system.' Would you like to see such an idea adopted in this country?" No wonder the responses were ambiguous! The question inextricably combined two separate ideas, choice among public schools and tax aid to nonpublic schools.

After receiving complaints over the years, Phi Delta Kappa and Gallup moved to separate the two ideas. In four polls between 1989 and 1993 the PDK/Gallup survey found support for choice among *public schools* ranging from 60 percent to 65 percent, with disapproval ranging from 31 percent to 33 percent.[2]

In 1993 Phi Delta Kappa/Gallup asked respondents: "Do you favor or oppose allowing students and parents to choose a private school to attend at public expense?" The result: 55 percent opposed, 45 percent in favor.[3] In 1995 the same question was used and the result was 65 percent opposed, 33 percent in favor, clearly a significant increase in opposition to vouchers.[4]

In the 1993 poll, by 63 percent to 34 percent respondents said that private schools accepting tax aid "should be accountable to public school authorities." Public school parents agreed 67 percent to 31 percent, while nonpublic school parents disagreed 57 percent to 40 percent.[5] In the 1995 poll, 73 percent of all respondents agreed.[6] The 1993 poll also showed that public school parents were more supportive of choice among public schools (68 percent to 31 percent) than were nonpublic school parents (61 percent to 38 percent).

The Phi Delta Kappa/Gallup polls also show that public schools enjoy far more public support than one would gather from all of the negative media coverage. The 1993 PDK/Gallup survey showed, for example, that 68 percent of public school parents rate the nation's public schools, in the aggregate, from average to excellent. However, when asked about public schools in their own communities, 84 percent of public and even 78 percent of nonpublic school parents rated public schools average to excellent. When asked to rate the school attended by their oldest child, 90 percent of parents judged them average to excellent.[7] The 1995 poll showed similar results: 65 percent of public school parents rated schools nationally OK to excellent, 83 percent so rated schools in their own communities, and 88 percent rated OK to excellent the school attended by their oldest child.[8]

As further evidence of the unpopularity of voucher plans, a California organization, the American Education Reform Foundation, announced on August 15, 1995, that it had decided to "pull the plug" on its effort to get another voucher initiative on the ballot in 1996. The group, backed by San Francisco billionaire and Wal-Mart store fortune heir John Walton, said that its polling data showed that Californians would very likely defeat the measure. Foundation president Eugene Ruffin said the group would mount an aggressive three-year propaganda campaign to change voters' minds and try to get vouchers on the ballot in 1998. Walton had reportedly been willing to spend $20 million or more to back the initiative.[9]

While Phi Delta Kappa/Gallup abandoned the ambiguous question they had used from 1970 through 1991, that question was used word for word by the Gallup Organization in 1993 for the National Catholic Educational Association, a group that favors and lobbies for vouchers. The result was claimed to show 70 percent to 27 percent support for vouchers. However, the Gallup Organization's Alec Gallup in a 1994 interview said:

> Our Lincoln [Nebraska] office conducted this NCEA poll without consulting me. And they made every mistake in the book. The worst was revealing the self-interest of the sponsoring organization in the question schedule that led up to the voucher question. The NCEA has long hoped for public money for the finan-

cially strapped Catholic school system. So poll context accounts largely for what is called, in polling parlance, "acquiescence": People tend to give you the answer they think you want.

Ideally, we would devote several questions to vouchers/choice in every Phi Delta Kappa poll to be sure we are assessing people's true feelings. Time does not always permit it. But we have asked a series of questions in two PDK polls since 1991, and I think we got the basic question right in the 1994 poll. It is stated thus: "A proposal has been made which would allow parents to send their school-age children to any public, private, or church-related school they choose. For parents choosing nonpublic schools, the government would pay all or part of the tuition. Would you favor or oppose this proposal in your state?"

On this question the division was 45 percent for and 54 percent against, with only 1 percent holding no opinion. I believe these percentages are an accurate reflection of sentiment, at this point in time, and I believe most people have pretty well made up their minds on the issue. The fact that so few were undecided in this poll is consistent with this conviction. Also, the findings are confirmed by the anti-voucher votes in Oregon, Colorado, and California in recent years.

Question wording is crucial, of course; we would probably have found even more than 54 percent opposition if we had said "government tax money" or "taxpayer's money." I am at last satisfied with question wording. If we use the question again next year, I predict that we will get a 45-55 split again, or very near it."[10]

Although Alec Gallup and Phi Delta Kappa like the 1994 question, we still consider it ambiguous and confusing. It still combines public school choice and nonpublic school vouchers in a single question, denying poll respondents the option of approving one and opposing the other. Further, the question suggests that parental choice is all that is needed to get a child into a nonpublic school, whereas in the real world it is generally the nonpublic school that chooses which children to admit and with what criteria. We believe that a properly worded question would elicit opposition on the order of two to one, just as voters made clear in the twenty state referenda, and just as Gallup found in the poll released on August 22, 1995.

Finally, a recent development in our neighbor to the north is of importance to the voucher debate in this country. On September 5, 1995, Newfoundlanders voted 54 percent to 46 percent to end church control over the Canadian province's schools, supporting popular Premier Clyde Wells' plan to consolidate the present system of church-controlled but tax-supported schools—in effect, a sort of voucher system—into a more efficient, less costly public school system. Students may receive religious instruction in released time classes held in public schools. At present there are separate Catholic, Pentecostal, Adventist, and Protestant (representing five denominations) schools under church control. Catholic Church officials opposed the change, but many Catholics voted for it.

The Toronto *Globe and Mail* praised the vote as an important step toward improving the province's "lamentable record of scholastic performance."

The vote is significant for several reasons. It marks the first time that a Canadian province's electorate has had an opportunity to vote on the question of tax support for separate denominational schools. And in view of the pressures in the United States to enact voucher plans for tax support of nonpublic schools, the Newfoundland vote marks a rejection of the basic voucher concept by a provincewide electorate that has never known any other form of schooling arrangement.

Notes

1. Stanley Elam, *How America Views Its Schools* (Bloomington, Ind.: Phi Delta Kappa Educational Foundation, 1995), pp. 51–54.

2. Ibid., pp. 55–59.

3. *Voice of Reason* (Americans for Religious Liberty newsletter) 46 (Summer 1993): 1, 6.

4. Stanley M. Elam and Lowell C. Rose, "The 27th Annual Poll of the Public Attitudes Toward the Public Schools," *Phi Delta Kappan* (September 1995): 46.

5. *Voice of Reason* 46: 1,6.

6. Elam and Rose, "The 27th Annual Poll," p. 46.

7. *Voice of Reason* 46: 1, 6.

8. Elam and Rose, "The 27th Annual Poll," pp. 42–43.

9. Richard Lee Colvin, "Pro-Voucher Group Delays Ballot Drive," *The Los Angeles Times*, August 16, 1995.

10. Elam, *How America Views Its Schools*, pp. 53–54.

3

Vouchers:
The Constitution Says No

Despite repeated and misleading claims to the contrary, vouchers are merely the latest in a long line of attempts by sectarian special interests to channel public money to church-related educational institutions. Vouchers, in whatever guise or form, are subsidies to religious education. They represent the transferral of tax funds to schools which inculcate distinctive denominational points of view, select teachers and other personnel who share those religious beliefs, and choose or attract their clientele largely on the basis of religious orientation. These are undeniable facts, and no amount of whitewashing can obliterate them.

Vouchers therefore will have to face constitutional tests, either at the federal level or, in some states, at the state level. Voucher legislation will inevitably clash with the U.S. constitutional prohibition known as the No Establishment Clause and with comparable provisions in state constitutions.

It may be appropriate at this point to look in some detail at the opening clause of the First Amendment: "Congress shall make no law respecting an establishment of religion. . . ." This explicit constitutional ban remains at the core of the juridical relationship between religion and government in the United States. Because of increasing intersections between church and state during the past half-century, this doctrine has taken on a unique life of its own. Hence, the phrase, "establishment clause doctrine" has become part of our legal language.

The classic definition of what "no establishment" means was handed down by the Supreme Court in a 1947 case concerning public support for parochial schools in New Jersey, *Everson* v. *Board of Education*:

> The "establishment of religion" clause of the First Amendment means at least this: neither the state nor the Federal Government can set up a church. Neither can pass laws which aid one religion, aid all religions, or prefer one religion over another. Neither can force nor influence a person to go or to remain away from church against his will or force him to profess a belief or disbelief in any religion. No person can be punished for entertaining or professing religious beliefs or disbeliefs, for church attendance or nonattendance. No tax in any amount, large or small, can be levied to support any religious activities or institutions, whatever they may be called, or whatever form they may adopt to teach or practice religion. Neither a state nor the Federal Government can, openly or secretly, participate in

the affairs of any religious organizations or groups and vice versa. In the words of Jefferson, the clause against establishment of religion by law was intended to erect "a wall of separation between church and state."[1]

A quarter of a century later, the High Court enunciated a three-part test in *Lemon* v. *Kurtzman*.[2] To pass constitutional scrutiny, legislation has to have a secular purpose, may not advance or inhibit religion, and may not result in "excessive entanglement" between church and state. It was with the *Lemon* test that the Supreme Court invalidated many attempts by lawmakers to provide tax aid to church-related elementary and secondary education. The test has also been applied to many questions surrounding religious activities in public education and disputes involving religious symbols on public property.

While the First Amendment prohibits the establishment of any kind of national religion (Justice William O. Douglas noted, "The First Amendment does not select any one group or any one type of religion for preferred treatment."[3]), the purpose of the adoption of the establishment clause was actually much more broad and far-reaching. Justice Wylie Rutledge observed:

The First Amendment's purpose was not to strike merely at the official establishment of a single sect, creed or religion, outlawing only a formal relation such as had prevailed in England and some of the colonies. Necessarily it was to uproot all such relationships. But the object was broader than separating church and state in this narrow sense. It was to create a complete and permanent separation of the spheres of religious activity and civil authority by comprehensively forbidding every form of public aid or support for religion.[4]

Justice Douglas argued that the Founders "fashioned a charter of government which envisaged the widest possible toleration of conflicting [religious] views."[5]

Furthermore, government cannot "suppress real or imagined attacks upon a particular religious doctrine,"[6] nor can it have any "interest in theology or ritual."[7]

Government may not prefer religion or religious persons over those who profess no religion. Justice Black wrote:

> We repeat and again reaffirm that neither a state nor the Federal Government can constitutionally force a person "to profess a belief or disbelief in any religion." Neither can constitutionally pass laws or impose requirements which aid all religions as against nonbelievers, and neither can aid those religions based on a belief in the existence of God as against those religions founded on different beliefs.[8]

Justice William J. Brennan affirmed, "The State must be steadfastly neutral in all matters of faith, and neither favor nor inhibit religion."[9]

Government may not "compose official prayers for any group of the American people to recite as part of a religious program carried on by government."[10]

The state may not "require that teaching and learning must be tailored to the principles or prohibitions of any religious sect or dogma,"[11] according to Justice Abe Fortas. In the same case Fortas also observed:

Government in our democracy, state and national, must be neutral in matters of religious theory, doctrine, and practice. It may not be hostile to any religion or to the advocacy of no religion; and it may not aid, foster, or promote one religion or religious theory against another or even against the militant opposite. The First Amendment mandates governmental neutrality between religion and religion, and between religion and nonreligion.[12]

Churches are "excluded from the affairs of government,"[13] said Chief Justice Warren E. Burger, and "important, discretionary governmental powers" may not be "delegated to or shared with religious institutions."[14]

Government may not "foster a close identification of its powers and responsibilities with those of any or all religious denominations,"[15] wrote Justice Brennan, who also noted that it is forbidden for legislation "to employ the symbolic and financial support of government to achieve a religious purpose."[16]

It should be noted that the Supreme Court has applied the establishment clause to the states through the Fourteenth Amendment since the *Everson* and *McCollum* cases in 1947 and 1948.

The Court has applied the *Lemon* test in several cases which specifically invalidated certain kinds of programs designed to aid church-related schools. It is important to note that failure to satisfy any one of the three points in *Lemon* will result in the invalidation of the legislation.

In 1973 the Court struck down a New York statute structured to give grants directly to parents for private school tuition reimbursement. In this case Justice Lewis

Powell, writing for the majority, observed: "By reimbursing parents for a portion of their tuition bill, the State seeks to relieve their financial burdens sufficiently to assure that they continue to have the option to send their children to religion-oriented schools. . . . The effect of the aid is unmistakably to provide desired financial support for nonpublic, sectarian institutions."[17] Furthermore, "If the grants are offered as an incentive to parents to send their children to sectarian schools by making unrestricted cash payments to them, the Establishment Clause is violated. Whether the grant is labeled a reimbursement, a reward or a subsidy, its substantive impact is still the same."[18]

The provision of various kinds of educational services and instructional materials to parochial schools by public authorities was held unconstitutional in 1973,[19] 1975,[20] and 1977.[21]

In 1985 the Court applied the test strictly to a Michigan school district, holding that state aid for even secular instruction in parochial schools still impermissibly advanced religion.[22]

It is true that the Supreme Court has moved away slightly from a strict application of the *Lemon* test. In some instances, following the lead of Justice Sandra O'Connor, the Court has modified it in the light of a new principle: the impact of the proposed legislation or activity on the equal status and political standing of religious minorities in the community.

It remains likely, however, that several key principles of the *Lemon* decision are still applicable. One concerns political divisiveness along religious lines. Chief Justice Burger explained the Court's concern: "Ordinarily, political debate and division, however vigorous or even partisan, are normal and healthy manifestations of our democratic system of government, but political division along religious lines was one of the principal evils against which the First Amendment was intended to protect. The potential divisiveness of such conflict is a threat to the normal political process."[23]

The Court echoed this warning in *Nyquist* when it observed that "aid programs of any kind tend to become entrenched, to escalate in cost, and to generate their own aggressive constituencies."[24]

Vouchers also have a tendency toward mixing or fusing ecclesiastical and political functions. Heller observes, "The Voucher Plan also impermissibly delegates the State's traditional responsibility for primary and secondary education to religious institutions. . . . Under the Voucher Plan, participating sectarian schools will wield unaccountable control over basic education—in effect, exercising an unacceptable veto power over school curricula, student admissions and teacher appointments."[25]

The excessive entanglement problem is inevitably involved in any voucher plan. Heller argues:

> The Voucher Plan will cause the State to become excessively entangled with religion because the State will have to administer and monitor the Voucher Plan. There are two facets to this involvement—the administration presently required under the Plan; and the administration that will inevitably arise from the Plan. Both may be considered under the authority of the *Lemon* decision.
>
> As a first step, government bureaucracy will be nec-

essary to issue and cash vouchers. As with other entitle-
ment programs, this will involve numerous verification
and reporting requirements. Parents and churches will
have to comply with a plethora of regulations to receive
government benefits—and the government will have to
amass information on both parents, children and
churches to issue and redeem vouchers. This arrangement gives the unmistakable imprimatur of state approval of religion because the government will be or-
ganizing, promoting and funding religious education.[26]

Another problem with voucher plans relates to the
fact that nonpublic schools tend to discriminate in admissions of students and hiring of teachers in ways prohib-
ited in public schools. In an important but seldom men-
tioned case in 1973, the Supreme Court examined a Mississippi law that provided textbook loans to nonpublic
school students. The Court held that since textbook loans
"are a form of tangible financial assistance benefitting the
schools themselves," equal protection guarantees are violated when the state furnishes textbooks to students in
private schools with racially discriminatory admission
policies. The Court stated: "A state's constitutional obligation requires it to steer clear not only of operating the old
dual system of racially segregated schools but also of giving significant aid to institutions that practice racial or
other invidious discrimination."[27] Nonpublic school
admissions and hiring policies that invidiously discriminate by race, ethnicity, religion, gender, or handicap
would raise serious questions about the constitutionality
of voucher aid to those institutions, and at the very least
would entangle government and sectarian schools imper-

missibly if efforts are made to police or regulate admissions and hiring policies.

Voucher plans may also violate state constitutions since many states have explicit prohibitions against any state aid to any religious institution. Twenty-four states ban any expenditure of public funds for parochial or sectarian education. Several states require that publicly supported education be religiously neutral. Some states maintain broad provisions against governmental partiality or preference toward religion in general. All fifty state constitutions have at least one basic provision protecting the religious liberty or liberty of conscience of its residents.

Here are some examples from state constitutions.

- Alabama, Article XIV, paragraph 263:

  No money raised for the support of the public schools shall be appropriated to or used for the support of any sectarian or denominational school.[28]

- Massachusetts, Article XVIII, Section 2:

  No grant, appropriation of the use of public money or property or loan of credit shall be made or authorized by the Commonwealth or any political subdivision thereof for the purpose of founding, maintaining or aiding any infirmary, hospital, institution, primary or secondary school, or charitable or religious undertaking which is not publicly owned and under the exclusive control, order and supervision of public officers or public agents authorized by the Commonwealth.[29]

- Michigan, Article VIII, Section 2:

  No public monies or property shall be appropriated or paid or any public credit utilized, by the legislature or any other political subdivision or agency of the state directly or indirectly to aid or maintain any private, denominational or other nonpublic preelementary, elementary, or secondary school. No payment, credit, tax benefit, exemption or deduction, tuition voucher, subsidy, grant or loan of public monies or property shall be provided, directly or indirectly, to support the attendance of any student or the employment of any person at any such nonpublic school or at any location or institution where instruction is offered in whole or in part to such nonpublic school students.[30]

- Missouri, Article IX, Section 8:

  Neither the general assembly, nor any county, city, town, township, school district or other municipal corporation, shall ever make an appropriation or pay from any public fund whatever, anything in aid of any religious creed, church or sectarian purpose or to help to support or sustain any private or public school, academy, seminary, college, university, or other institution of learning controlled by any religious creed, church or sectarian denomination whatever; nor shall any grant or donation of personal property or real estate ever be made by the state, or any county, city, town, or other municipal corporation, for any religious creed, church, or sectarian purpose whatever.[31]

• North Dakota, Article VIII, Section 152:

> No money raised for the support of the public
> schools of the state shall be appropriated to or used
> for support of any sectarian school.[32]

The existence of these state provisions is relevant to
the voucher debate because the U.S. Supreme Court
ruled in a 1980 case that states may interpret their own
constitutions more strictly than the federal Constitution,
as long as there is no direct conflict between a federal law
and a state statute.[33]

Several state supreme courts, including those of California, Minnesota, and Washington, have interpreted
their constitutional provisions strictly in order to limit
state subsidies for religion and to protect their citizens
from acts tending toward religious establishment.[34]

A recent decision by the Puerto Rico Supreme Court
reveals that state constitutions can be interpreted to limit
vouchers or other parochiaid schemes. In 1994 the
Puerto Rico Supreme Court invalidated a voucher program as a violation of Article 2, Section 5, of the commonwealth's constitution. This voucher proposal had
mandated $1,500 vouchers for private and parochial
schools. The plan initially cost $2.7 million.[35]

While vouchers clearly fail on their public policy merits, they are also likely to result in numerous legal challenges from taxpayers who believe that such expenditures
from the public treasury are unconstitutional.

Notes

1. 330 U.S. 15, 16.

2. 403 U.S. 602.

3. *United States* v. *Ballard*, 322 U.S. 86, 87 (1944).

4. *Everson* v. *Board of Education*, 330 U.S. 31, 32 (1947).

5. 322 U.S. 87.

6. *Burstyn* v. *Wilson*, 343 U.S. 495 (1952).

7. *McGowan* v. *Maryland*, 366 U.S. 563, 564 (1961).

8. *Torcaso* v. *Watkins*, 367 U.S. 495 (1961).

9. *Abington School District* v. *Schempp*, 374 U.S. 226, 229 (1963).

10. *Engel* v. *Vitale*, 370 U.S. 425 (1962).

11. *Epperson* v. *Arkansas*, 393 U.S. 106 (1968).

12. 393 U.S. 103, 104.

13. *Lemon* v. *Kurtzman*, 403 U.S. 602, 625 (1975).

14. *Larkin* v. *Grendel's Den*, 459 U.S. 127 (1982).

15. *Grand Rapids School District* v. *Ball*, 473 U.S. 373 (1985).

16. *Edwards* v. *Aguillard*, 482 U.S. 578 (1987).

17. *Committee for Public Education* v. *Nyquist*, 413 U.S. 756 (1973).

18. Ibid.

19. *Levitt* v. *Committee for Public Education and Religious Liberty*, 413 U.S. 472 (1973).

20. *Meek* v. *Pittinger*, 421 U.S. 349 (1975).

21. *Wolman* v. *Walters*, 433 U.S. 229 (1977).

22. *Grand Rapids* v. *Ball*, 473 U.S. 373 (1985).

23. *Lemon* v. *Kurtzman*, 403 U.S. 602, 622 (1971).

24. *Committee for Public Education and Religious Liberty* v. *Nyquist*, 413 U.S. 756, 796 (1973).

25. David Heller, ed., *Education Vouchers* (New York: The National Committee for Public Education and Religious Liberty, 1995), p. 14.

26. Ibid., pp. 12–13.

27. *Norwood* v. *Harrison,* 93 S.Ct. 2804 (1973).

28. Edd Doerr and Albert J. Menendez, *Religious Liberty and State Constitutions* (Amherst, N.Y.: Prometheus Books, 1993), p. 19.

29. Ibid., p. 50.

30. Ibid., p. 52.

31. Ibid., p. 57.

32. Ibid., p. 73.

33. *Pruneyard Shopping Center* v. *Robins,* 477 U.S. 74 (1980). See also *Garnett* v. *Renton School Dist.,* 987 F.2d 641 (9th Cir. 1991) and *Michigan* v. *Long,* 463 U.S. 1032 (1983).

34. See *Witters* v. *State Commission for the Blind,* 771 P.2d 1119 (Wash. 1989).

35. *Asociacion de Maestros de Puerto Rico* v. *Torres* (Supreme Court of Puerto Rico, 1994 W. L. 780744).

4

The Nature of Nonpublic Schools

No meaningful discussion of voucher plans to aid or support nonpublic schools can ignore the nature of those schools. In sharp contrast to our democratically controlled and religiously neutral public schools, nonpublic schools are in the main pervasively sectarian institutions (at least 85 percent of nonpublic enrollment) that appeal necessarily to denominationally narrow constituencies. In this chapter we will examine the main types of religious nonpublic schools.

Fundamentalist and Protestant Schools

While Catholic school enrollment has shrunk from 5.5 million students to about half that figure since 1965,

there has been a significant growth in Protestant fundamentalist school enrollment.

Fundamentalist schools are perhaps the most committed to religious orthodoxy. In his ethnographic study
of a Midwestern fundamentalist Christian school, Alan
Peshkin argues that such schools are all-encompassing,
totalistic institutions that seek to mold individuals in
accordance with a unitary approach to life. The school he
studied, Bethany Baptist Academy, was "a total institution,
the natural organizational outcome of a school based on
absolute truth."[1] Peshkin explained that the school's published purposes, and those of the American Association
of Christian Schools, are decidedly sectarian. They are: to
bring children to salvation; to inform children about the
Word of God; to keep children immersed in God; to keep
children separate from the world; to encourage children
to proselytize the unsaved; to lead children into service as
preachers, teachers, and evangelists; and to have children
become fully committed Christians, living their lives first
and foremost for the glory of God.[2]

Peshkin also found that the academy's teachers and
principal conceive their roles as more missionary than
academic. He found that secular and religious values
interacted and reinforced each other. He was also dis-
turbed that the school's narrow approach to religion
would lead many of its graduates to live their entire lives
in religious ghettoes and to regard those of other faiths as
threats to their existence rather than as neighbors and
friends.

Additional studies corroborate Peshkin's analysis.
Paul A. Kienel, executive director of the Association of
Christian Schools International, a federation of Ameri-

can evangelical schools, asserted uncompromisingly in 1977 that "Christian schools are Christian institutions, where Jesus Christ and the Bible are central in the school curriculum and in the lives of teachers and administrators."[3]

Mississippi State University Professor James C. Carper, in his study of Christian separate schools, explained this burgeoning phenomenon.

> Since the mid-1960s, evangelical Protestants and their churches have been establishing Christian day schools at a phenomenal rate. Several proponents of these institutions have claimed, perhaps with some exaggeration, that Christian schools are being established at the rate of nearly two per day. Not only do these schools currently constitute the most rapidly expanding segment of formal education in the United States, but they also represent the first widespread secession from the public school pattern since the establishment of Catholic schools in the nineteenth century.[4]

Carper adds: "Studies of the reasons parents send their children to such schools point consistently to their desire for a Christ-centered or Bible-centered academic program."[5]

Carper states that while these schools vary widely in academic quality, social status, equipment, and course offerings, they share a central viewpoint. He says: "Although these institutions are diverse in many respects, they all profess the centrality of Jesus Christ and the Bible in their educational endeavors. Regardless of the subject matter, a conservative Christian perspective is usually employed."[6] (Albert J. Menendez has made an extensive study of the textbooks used in fundamentalist schools. His findings are presented in Chapter 5.)

Protestant schools, especially those representing the more conservative evangelical and fundamentalist churches, have been growing and attracting more students since the 1970s. Some of them belong to associations like the National Association of Christian Schools. Older established evangelical churches also maintain separate schools, including the National Union of Christian Schools, representing the Christian Reformed Church, and the substantial school system maintained by the Lutheran Church Missouri Synod. Seventh-day Adventists, Jews, Episcopalians, Mennonites, Quakers, Amish, mainline Muslims, Greek and Russian Orthodox Christians, independent Baptists, Hare Krishnas, the Transcendental Meditation movement, and the Nation of Islam also maintain private schools. (There are also several hundred thousand students attending elite prep schools and military academies, many of them belonging to the National Association of Independent Schools.)

Religion clearly permeates the various Protestant school systems, both in philosophy and content of instruction.

Professor Harry C. Coiner of Concordia Theological Seminary describes Missouri Synod Lutheran schools as follows:

> The church-related school, which does not face the problem of religious pluralism and is free to teach Biblical doctrines, can do much more specific work in Christian education.

The [Lutheran] school enables the child to experience a totally Christ-centered program, a program which focuses the application of God's word on him and on all areas of his life.

The relationship of science, social studies, language, arithmetic, and other subjects to Biblical truth may be taught without limitation.

Daily social contact between teachers and pupils of the same Christian faith reinforces learning by attitude and example. The absence of any formal educational influence that is strange, foreign, or antagonistic in any way to the positive Christian educational process permits the building of one stone on another without destructive influence.[7]

In their book *The Amish School,* Sara E. Fisher and Rachel K. Stahl observe that "religion is taught all day long in the lessons and on the playground. The goal of the Amish schools is to prepare children for usefulness by preparing them for eternity. Each morning, devotions are held. The Bible is read and the Lord's Prayer is repeated in unison."[8] Amish schools reflect and are pervaded by Amish values. "An Amish child is not taught to have selfish needs of privacy, space, recognition and admiration, ambition and rewards that a child in large society absorbs as its birthright."[9] They are not encouraged to study beyond the eighth grade. "An Amish child has an enormous sense of security in community. Leaving that security for the fleeting pleasure of higher education is not only risky but fearsome for most."[10]

Textbooks are carefully selected. Since 1948 the Old Order Book Society in Lancaster County, Pennsylvania, has reprinted textbooks long since discarded by public schools but considered "wholesome" by the Amish.[11] Fisher and Stahl maintain that "much of the secular school curricula taught evolution, technology, sex education, and other values contrary to Amish belief."[12]

All church-related schools cite religious belief and practice as major factors in the decision to maintain separate educational institutions. A Seventh-day Adventist educator has observed, "Seventh-day Adventist education is basically a church-supported program. Aside from the tuition and fees paid by students and their parents, the bulk of the financial support comes from the local churches and supporting organizations."[13] He continues:

> The public schools cannot provide teachers who can teach their disciplines and at the same time relate them to religion and religious life. . . . Adventists believe that their young people must not only be trained and educated to live and to make a contribution in this world, but they must also be readied for the great Advent, and of course there are other approaches that could not be taken in a public system but which would be quite common in a Christian school.
>
> Every school system must have specific goals and objectives. Those of the Seventh-day Adventist schools include the development of the spiritual or religious which are paramount and which must permeate the pupils' total program. They must demonstrate a good understanding of the Scriptures and be knowledgeable in the doctrines of the church.[14]

Professor George R. Knight of Andrews University describes his church's school system.

Adventism has developed a curricular stance that is unashamedly based on biblical revelation and looks at science from the standpoint of creationism. Adventists hold that all truth is essentially religious, and some contemporary educators have given great impetus and publicity to the techniques of integrating all subject matter within the context and worldview of the Bible. The General Conference Department of Education has been active in developing textbooks in such areas as science, reading, social studies, and religion in an attempt to better present the Christian perspective in every classroom subject.[15]

Another type of conservative Protestant school educates about 75,000 students of largely Dutch ancestry in the American Midwest, particularly in Iowa and Michigan. These are the Calvinist-oriented National Union of Christian Schools International, based in Grand Rapids, Michigan. A study of these schools concluded that their unifying feature was "a grounding in biblical/theological principles as seen in Calvinist perspective."[16] Furthermore, "the leaders and spokesmen have over the years forged a web of interrelated doctrines which provide the religious foundations of the movement."[17]

Two values shape these schools, say Opperval and De Boer. "The proper relation between education and religion is not that of neutrality toward all, nor simple indoctrination in one, but the integration of a religious worldview into all curriculum content. The aim of such education is neither evangelization for church membership nor neutral, value-free information-giving, but preparing the learner for living a Christian lifestyle in contemporary society."[18] Calvinist schools also have as a goal "helping young Christians to exercise cultural dominion rather than seeking cultural isolation."[19] Calvinist school text-books reflect these values and concerns. Opperval and De Boer reveal that religious interpretations permeate all courses, from civics to science to biology, health education, and literature.

Roman Catholic Schools

About 2.6 million students attend Catholic schools, down from 5.5 million in 1965. While Catholic schools once enrolled about 85 percent of nonpublic students, they now enroll only about half. As white Catholics now have higher average incomes than white Protestants, the decline in enrollment is based less on economic than other factors. The election of a Catholic President in 1960, the Supreme Court's 1962–63 school prayer rulings, and the liberalizing influence of the Second Vatican Council all helped make public education more attractive to Catholics, while widespread discomfort with post-Vatican Council stands on contraception, marriage, abortion, clerical celibacy, and ordination of women made parochial schools less attractive.

Catholic schools exist primarily to inculcate a distinctive religious value system that is clearly denominational. This should be apparent from the foundation of Catholic education and its place in church law. The revised Code of Canon Law, promulgated by Pope John Paul II in 1983, enumerates the official Catholic principles of education.

• Canon 794: "The duty and right of educating belongs in a unique way to the Church which has been divinely entrusted with the mission to assist men and women so that they can arrive at the fullness of the Christian life. Pastors of souls have the duty to arrange all things so that all the faithful may enjoy a Catholic education."[20] Coriden comments that this canon "grounds the Church's duty and right to educate on a supernatural warrant alone, . . ."[21]

• Canon 798: "Parents are to entrust their children to those schools in which Catholic education is provided; but if they are unable to do this, they are bound to provide for their suitable Catholic education outside the schools."[22]

• Canon 803: "It is necessary that the formation and education given in a Catholic school be based upon the principles of Catholic doctrine; teachers are to be outstanding for their correct doctrine and integrity of life."[23] Paragraph 3 adds, "Even if it really be Catholic, no school may bear the title Catholic school without the consent of the competent ecclesiastical authority."[24]

Coriden comments:

Among the many possible criteria of a school's Catholicity, e.g., name recognition, origin, stated purpose, ownership, operating authority, faith commitment of teachers or students, spirit and atmosphere, orthodox teaching, or actual inculcation of gospel values, the Code has chosen what is perhaps the simplest and most verifiable criterion: operation or recognition by church authority. . . . [B]oth the formation (of character) and education in a Catholic school is to be grounded upon the basics of Catholic teaching, and . . . the teachers are to be outstanding for their correct teaching and moral probity."[25]

• Canon 804: "Catholic religious formation and education which are imparted in any schools whatsoever as well as that acquired through the various media of social communications are subject to the authority of the Church; . . ."[26]

Several specialists reiterate and explain these principles.

The Rev. John L. McKenzie, professor of theology at the University of Notre Dame, says:

The Roman Catholic schools have always placed religious education as the primary purpose of the schools with no attempt to mask this under some other purpose. . . . The principle on which church education is conducted goes far beyond formal religious instruction. Children also learn the way of worship; they are taught respect and reverence for prelates, clergy, and religious. They are daily reminded of their identity as Catholics. They grow up in an atmosphere of Roman Catholic traditions and attitudes which are communicated not so much by instruction as by prolonged close association under the direction of professional religious persons.[27]

The Rev. Neil G. McCluskey, formerly dean of teacher education at Lehman College at City University of New York, notes that religion pervades the Catholic school curriculum, "particularly in literature, history, and the social studies." He adds that, "The function of the Catholic school is not merely to teach the formulas of the Catholic religion but . . . 'to impart in a thousand ways, which defy formularization, the Catholic attitude toward life as a whole.' "[28]

In principle, Catholic schools are pervasively religious institutions. "Every subject taught," said Pope Pius XI in 1929, quoting his predecessor Leo XIII, "(should) be permeated with Christian piety."[29] Permeation, then, is the ideal for Catholic schools, which "propose many Christian values to the students, aboveboard and out in the open, in subject area and in co-curricular activities, in liturgies and other religious celebrations."[30]

Pedagogical literature and court rulings on various forms of tax aid to Catholic schools show that Catholic schools in both theory and practice are pervasively religious institutions operating within a specific denominational tradition, institutions whose programs are permeated by religious, and often narrowly denominational, values, teachings, and doctrines. This fact has been examined and acknowledged by the highest court in the land.

The governance of Catholic schools reflects this religious orientation. The faculties of Catholic schools have a substantially religious mission, one tied inseparably to a particular denomination and even more specifically to the more orthodox positions of that denomination's hierarchy. Teachers in Catholic schools understand and support that mission.

Catholic school student bodies differ markedly from those of public schools. While the religious composition

of the public school student population is quite diverse—
representing literally every religious persuasion, including about three-fourths of U.S. Catholic children of
school age (Catholics make up about 23 percent of the
U.S. population and about 19 percent of the public
school student population)—Catholic school enrollment
tends strongly toward religious homogeneity. According
to statistics from the National Catholic Educational Association, 92.9 percent of the non-African American students in Catholic elementary and secondary schools are
Catholic; of the 9 percent of enrollment which is African
American, two-thirds are reported to be non-Catholic.[31]
That the overwhelming majority of white, Hispanic, and
Asian students in Catholic schools are Catholic is unques-
tionably due to the fact that the schools are pervasively
denominational schools and are so perceived by anyone
who looks at them.

Information on Catholic schools relevant to the
voucher debate may be found in *Catholic Schools: The Facts*,
by Edd Doerr (Americans for Religious Liberty, 1993).

Jewish Schools

Orthodox Jewish schools have a clear religious identity
and purpose. Eduardo Rauch says that Jewish schools
adhere to the following eight educational objectives: to
provide knowledge of the classical Jewish texts and the
traditions embodied therein; to foster a lifelong commitment to the study of Torah; to develop some form of personal observance; to develop a facility in the Hebrew language and a familiarity with its literature; to nurture an

identification with the Jewish people through a knowledge of its past, and to encourage a concern for its survival and welfare the world over; to stimulate a recognition of the unique place of Israel in the Jewish imagination, both past and present, and to foster the acceptance of some sort of personal obligation to participate in its development; to encourage participation in American society, based on a conscious awareness of the relationship between Jewish tradition and democracy; to inculcate faith in God and trust in his beneficence.[32]

Rauch also points out that "most [Jewish] schools include subjects such as prayer, the first five books of the Bible, learned comments to these five books by the medieval scholar Rashi, prophets, Hebrew language, arts, laws and customs, history, sections of the Talmud, ethics and Israel."[33] Finally, he notes, "One of the basic features of the day school program is pupil participation in religious activities. . . . Experiences around the religious holidays are regularly planned."[34]

Ari L. Goldman, the religion correspondent of the *New York Times*, describes his education at an Orthodox yeshiva in New York City:

> At the right-wing Orthodox high school I attended, there was no acknowledgment that anyone but us, sitting there poring over the Talmud, had any religious validity. Christianity was unmentionable. . . . We were also taught to shun those in the more liberal Reformed and Conservative branches of Judaism. Just as one was not permitted to enter a church (even if only to escape the rain), one could not walk into a Reform or Conservative Temple.[35]

Goldman says that school authorities saw religious knowledge as far more important than secular culture.

> Likewise, so-called secular knowledge—math, science, literature—was given second-class status. "Real" knowledge was knowledge of the Torah; the rest was only a concession to a world into which we would have to go out someday and make a living. College was frowned upon, although the right-wing rabbis looked the other way if you studied Torah during the day and went to college at night.[36]

Notes

1. Alan Peshkin, *God's Choice: The Total World of a Fundamentalist Christian School* (Chicago: University of Chicago Press, 1986), p. 258.

2. Ibid., p. 259.

3. *Christian School Comment*, 1977, p. 1.

4. James C. Carper, "The Christian Day School," in *Religious Schooling in America*, ed. James C. Carper and Thomas C. Hunt (Birmingham, Ala.: Religious Education Press, 1984), p. 111.

5. Ibid., p. 118.

6. Ibid.

7. Victoria C. Krause, ed., *Lutheran Elementary Schools in Action* (St. Louis, Mo.: Concordia Press, 1963), p. 17.

8. Sara E. Fisher and Rachel K. Stahl, *The Amish School* (Intercourse, Pa.: Good Books, 1986), p. 4.

9. Ibid., p. 88.

10. Ibid., pp. 90, 91.

11. Ibid., p. 43.

12. Ibid., p. 40.

13. Charles B. Hirsch, "Seventh-day Adventist Education," *Church & State* 24 (April 1971): 8.

14. Ibid., p. 9.

15 . George R. Knight, "Seventh-day Adventist Education," in Carper and Hunt, *Religious Schooling in America*, p. 103.

16. Donald Opperval and Peter P. De Boer, "Calvinist Day Schools," in Carper and Hunt, *Religious Schooling in America*, p. 73.

17. Ibid.

18. Ibid., p. 74.

19. Ibid., p. 76.

20. James A. Coriden, Thomas J. Green, and Donald E. Heintschel, eds., *The Code of Canon Law: A Text and Commentary* (New York: Paulist Press, 1985).

21. Ibid., p. 565.

22. Ibid., p. 566.

23. Ibid., p. 568.

24. Ibid., p. 568.

25. Ibid., p. 568.

26. Ibid., p. 568.

27. John L. McKenzie, *The Roman Catholic Church* (New York: Doubleday and Co., 1971), pp. 294–95.

28. Neil G. McCluskey, *Catholic Viewpoint on Education* (New York: Doubleday and Co., 1962), pp. 74, 78.

29. Edwin J. McDermott, *Distinctive Qualities of the Catholic School* (Washington, D.C.: National Catholic Educational Association, 1990), p. 51.

30. Ibid., p. 50.

31. Michael J. Guerra, *Lighting New Fires: Catholic Schooling in America 25 Years After Vatican II* (Washington, D.C.: National Catholic Educational Association, 1991), pp. 5–7.

32. Eduardo Rauch, "The Jewish Day School in America," in Carper and Hunt, *Religious Schooling in America*, p. 133. See

also Walter I. Ackerman, "Jewish Education—For What?" *American Jewish Yearbook* 70 (1969): 17–18.

33. Ibid., p. 144.

34. Ibid., p. 145.

35. Ari L. Goldman, *The Search for God at Harvard* (New York: Random House, 1991), p. 103.

36. Ibid.

5

Fundamentalist Textbooks:
Teaching Bigotry

America's fastest-growing school movement during the past two decades has been the fundamentalist Christian day school and its closely related ally, the home schooling movement. Fueled by a discontent toward the increasingly multicultural and religiously pluralistic public schools, these sectarian separatist schools aim at insulating their students from modern life and culture.

Their primary *raison d'être* is a desire to protect their youth from the diversity of contemporary American society. This is accomplished intellectually by the textbooks developed for use in these schools.

The two primary textbook publishers for the nondenominational fundamentalist schools are Bob Jones University Press in Greenville, South Carolina, and Pensacola Christian College Press in Pensacola, Florida. The world view they promote is distinctive and quite unlike the values, attitudes. and historical interpretations of mainstream textbook publishers.

These texts promote sectarian separation, religious intolerance, anti-intellectualism, disdain for the scientific spirit, and right-wing political extremism. But it is in the area of religion that these texts are most reprehensible and judgmental.

In their book *The American Republic for Christian Schools*,[1] Rachel C. Larson and Pamela Creason set the tone when they call America today "a society where God is commonly rejected,"[2] though 95 percent of Americans say they believe in a Supreme Being and even though Americans have a higher church attendance rate than any other large industrial nation.

Attacks on all religious traditions other than conservative Protestantism are routine and pervasive. Raymond St. John's *American Literature for Christian Schools*[3] condemns religious pluralism forthrightly: "All these false versions of true religion and worship contribute to the growing theological anarchy of a nation whose people do merely what seems right in their own eyes."[4]

Religious liberalism, according to Larson and Creason, "hardened many Americans in their sin,"[5] while St. John affirms, "Religious liberalism is only a modern form of the paganism of Christ's day."[6] Christian Scientists, Seventh-day Adventists and Mormons are called "cults that denied Biblical truths."[7] Unitarianism, in Michael Lowman's *United States History in Christian Perspective*,[8] is labeled a "false religion" which "ignored man's need for forgiveness of sin through the blood of Christ and said that men should simply follow the teachings of Jesus and the dictates of their own reason."[9] Larson and Creason call Unitarianism "an unbelieving religion"[10] and "an unBiblical philosophy."[11] Eastern Orthodox Christians teach "beliefs contrary to Scripture"[12] and "have virtually turned icons into objects of worship."[13]

Episcopalians and Anglicans receive constant criticism in history and literature texts. Anglicans and Episcopalians are repeatedly denounced as effete, corrupt, and much too Catholic in these fundamentalist school texts. Ronald Horton's *British Literature for Christian Schools: The Modern Tradition, 1688 to the Present*[14] sets the tone when he says the Anglican Church is "dead in ritualism and rationalism and serves mainly a ceremonial function."[15]

David A. Fisher's *World History for Christian Schools* blames Jews for the crucifixion of Jesus. "The Jewish religious leaders, whose blindness and hypocrisy Jesus had denounced, sought to put Him to death. They brought Christ before the Roman governor Pontius Pilate, charging that Christ had disrupted the state. . . . Although Pilate found no fault in Jesus, he desired to maintain the peace. Giving in to the Jewish demands, he sentenced Jesus to death by crucifixion."[16]

Muslims, Buddhists, and Hindus are also ridiculed.

But the *bête noire* of fundamentalist textbook writers is the Roman Catholic Church. In the history, literature, geography, and science texts, Catholic-bashing is an acceptable and seemingly indispensable method of instruction.

In world history the students are only informed about the features of Catholic faith, culture, and practice which are deemed objectionable or heretical by fundamentalists. There is no attempt made to understand the historical development of Christianity, or the mutations which it underwent as it emerged from Palestine to become the dominant force and culture of European civilization.

The student learns nothing about the writings of early church fathers, the rise of the Papacy, the conflicts between church and state, the development of religious calendars and holy days, basilica architecture, theological controversies, the development of a cult of honor accorded to martyrs and confessors, liturgy, or church government. What is taught is essentially caricature.

Fisher calls Catholicism "a perversion of biblical Christianity,"[17] claims that Catholic leaders are "blinded by superstition and ignorance,"[18] as they control a church "sunk deep in moral corruption."[19] "During the fifteenth and sixteenth centuries," Glen Chambers and Gene Fisher say, "the Roman church destroyed more Bibles than the pagan emperors had destroyed during the first five centuries of church history. Thus, the Roman Catholic system ensured the people's intellectual and spiritual ignorance by depriving them of God's infallible Word and placing in their hands instead the traditions of fallible men."[20]

Chambers and Fisher portray the French and Indian War as a "war for religious freedom" and an effort "to preserve a biblical Protestantism in America."[21] The same text makes the absurd charge that one factor in the Civil War was the South's desire to retain its Protestant identity.[22]

This text says: "Immigration aggravated labor unrest"[23] and "immigrants were widely resented, for a number of reasons."[24] The main reason was that "many immigrants, especially those from southeastern Europe, were Roman Catholic, a fact that aroused fear and resentment among Protestants and others who feared the potential political power of the Roman church."[25]

In Lowman's U.S. history, Catholicism is described as "a distorted Christianity that had largely departed from the teachings of the Bible."[26] Chambers and Fisher are also blunt: "Catholicism enslaves man. From this corrupted system emerged the Roman Catholic Church."[27]

Students who receive their entire educational experience in schools which use these books will absorb visions of reality that are abhorrent to the vast majority of Americans, especially to those whose religious traditions and convictions are slandered and distorted.

William S. Pinkston, Jr.'s *Biology for Christian Schools*[28] admits at the beginning, "The people who have prepared this book have tried consistently to put the Word of God first and science second."[29] This negative attitude toward science pervades the text. Students are urged to disregard facts and conclusions widely held in the scientific community. "If the conclusions contradict the Word of God, the conclusions are wrong no matter how many scientific facts may appear to back them."[30]

A negative bias against science itself appears early on and is linked with the fatalism and acceptance of human imperfectability that pervades the whole Bob Jones University series. Thus we are told, "There will be sickness, suffering, and death until Christ returns for His thousand-year reign on the earth. Man must now earn his bread by the sweat of his brow because of God's curse upon the earth. The Bible teaches that things are getting worse and that God is the source of all that is good."[31] The scientific method is seen as limited. "It is important for the Christian to realize what science is and the limitations of science so that he can see the proper relationship between science, God, and His Word."[32] Also, "Although some people attribute godlike capabilities to science, science is actually little more than what man can sense around him."[33] Finally, "Not only does science have many limitations, but also man is a sinful creature and cannot perfectly rule the earth,"[34] and "It is wrong for a Christian to think that scientific achievements will replace faith in God . . . science cannot save a man from hell."[35]

Evolution is repeatedly condemned, and Christians are warned that they must reject it. Christians who accept evolution are not true Christians because "One must believe all the Word of God or believe none of it."[36] Further,

> A person who believes that God directed evolutionary processes is a theistic evolutionist and is in error. When the Bible states one thing and, in an attempt to be scientific, a person believes something else, he is setting up scientific theory as more authoritative than the Word of God. . . . A person who rejects any portion of the Bible has placed himself above the Bible. The Bible is accurate in *everything*.[37]

This text affirms that the world, for example, can be no more than 10,000 years old. In conclusion, students are told: "Biblical creationism is accepted by faith. A creationist, however, should not feel that science contradicts his faith in God's Word. Rather than being disproved by science the Scriptural concept of a young earth is actually verified by science."[38]

Pinkston's second volume for biology courses continues in the same vein, telling students that "Satan is in control of the physical world around us."[39]

A fatalistic world view can be seen in this phrase, "War is not a desirable event, but in this world it is often necessary."[40]

Pinkston roundly condemns hypnosis, sleeping medicine, and psychology. "The Bible teaches us that God controls sickness and health and works His will through both. Sometimes He accomplishes His will through healing, other times through death. . . . If God wants to heal miraculously He will."[41]

Sexual behavior is linked to disease and divine retribution. God "demands sexual purity"[42] and sexual sins "are a transgression of God's commandment and defile the body and mind."[43] Therefore, "The diseases that may result are a reminder that God punishes sinners."[44]

Abortion is "the killing of an unborn child."[45] It can never be acceptable. "People may try to redefine the terms and may pass laws to the contrary, but abortion is killing a human—and that is murder."[46] There are no exceptions, even for probable physical deformity. "God has ordained what we call handicapped or deformed. When it comes to deliberately killing a human that we feel is not physically or mentally 'normal,' we are ignoring the Bible's teaching about the sovereignty of God and the sanctity of human life."[47] Nothing is said about rape or the possibility of the mother's death.

Rejection of biological evolution is a keystone in several fundamentalist textbooks. Chambers and Fisher say, "Darwin's theory, or modifications of it, have gained wide acceptance, despite the fact that the key premises are unsupported by scientific law or investigation. . . . The main selling point for evolution is not that it has abundant support, but that it explains the universe without referring to God, and so it relieves man of any responsibility to his Creator."[48] Michael R. Lowman echoes this assessment. The discoveries of Charles Darwin are called "pseudo-scientific ideas" which "tore away the moral foundation of the European nations."[49] Raymond A. St. John claims that "Darwin's *Origin of Species* brought more attacks against the Word of God than did any other source."[50]

Related to this disdain for science is a pervasive anti-intellectualism. In subtle and not-so-subtle ways, students are warned against pursuing the life of the mind. They are constantly told that the intellectual leaders of society, writers and scientists especially, are often in the forefront of apostate movements that challenge or deny the Gospel. Even clergy are more likely to betray the faith than the simple-minded laity. Secular colleges and universities are portrayed as centers of apostasy, as in this reference from Chambers and Fisher: "Because colleges tend to exalt knowledge and reason above faith, they are often the first social institution to experience religious decline."[51]

These texts express ambivalence toward religious liberty, glorify the Puritans, exaggerate the historical significance of revivalism, and wax eloquent over Prohibition. They tend to ignore or disparage the achievements of African-Americans and Native Americans.

The treatment of Dr. Martin Luther King, Jr., is far from friendly. Chambers and Fisher write:

Because he couched his speeches in peaceful termi-
nology, he gained a reputation as a man of peace; he
was even awarded the Nobel Peace Prize in 1964. . . .
King had become a symbol of civil rights; his death
brought violence and destruction in several parts of the
country. Like Kennedy, he was viewed by many as a
martyr for human rights; his increasing shift to the left,
especially in the last year of his life, was soon forgot-
ten.[52]

The Civil Rights movement of the 1960s is dismissed:

Encouraged by Kennedy's promise of support, Negroes
began demanding equal social rights. . . . During
Kennedy's administration civil rights leaders made
steps toward gaining better treatment for Negroes, but
the demonstrations increased hatred and bitterness
among many. . . . As violence increased, the leadership
of civil rights organizations became more militant.[53]

Chambers and Fisher also remind students that "the
Bible does not specifically condemn slavery."[54]
The same volume has this to say about the religions of
Native Americans:

The concept of sin was foreign to the Indian culture;
discipline was intended to teach children to survive
rather than to make them moral. This amoral philosophy was often discouraging to Christian missionaries,
who found it difficult to teach Indians the difference
between right and wrong. . . . The Indian culture typified heathen civilization—lost in darkness without the
light of the gospel.[55]

Larson and Creason contribute this gem: "The Indians who terrorized the miners and cowboys terrorized the settlers too. Disgruntled over the loss of their lands and the destruction of the buffalo, the Indians were quick to go on the rampage."[56]

These texts have their own version of political correctness: Ultraconservative and far-right. Those who study American history in fundamentalist schools receive a novel view of our nation's political development. They are told that every Democratic president departed from constitutional principles of limited government, instead preferring to advance the behemoth of the secular state and a socialist economic system. Even those presidents universally regarded by historians as great or near great receive short shrift. Consider Franklin Roosevelt.

FDR, still an admired and beloved figure to average Americans and historians alike, is labeled a failure in texts used in most conservative Protestant schools. David A. Fisher writes, "In retrospect the New Deal, as Roosevelt's programs were called, did more harm than good. . . . Roosevelt's policies, which were often ill-planned and experimental, increased government spending and the power of the federal bureaucracy."[57]

Larson and Creason reiterate this theme. "The New Deal was giving the federal government wide powers over industry and commerce, areas that were not government's rightful sphere. Roosevelt's agencies were replacing the free enterprises of capitalism with the government regulations of socialism."[58]

Chambers and Fisher admire Senator Joseph McCarthy. "Many of his accusations were indeed true . . . but the liberal media soon discredited him."[59]

John F. Kennedy's death is treated with sarcasm. "His popularity had been declining rapidly. Civil rights leaders were not satisfied with his support of their programs; liberal leaders sought greater federal spending; conservative leaders were especially concerned by his failures in foreign affairs. Yet after his assassination, he became the virtual hero of the age."[60]

The Vietnam War is praised and the U.S. defeat blamed on the liberal media. "Limitations placed on U.S. military personnel by their own government, held virtually hostage by a hostile press and the constant threat of riots, made winning the war impossible."[61]

Michael Lowman's American history volume praises J. Edgar Hoover because he "understood the importance of maintaining America's traditional moral values."[62]

Labor unions are repeatedly condemned in these history and civics texts. Chambers and Fisher are emphatic in their claim that "Most of the major labor strikes in our history have been immoral."[63]

These books wax eloquent when discussing Republican Presidents who also had evangelical religious convictions, i.e, "great" leaders like Garfield, Harrison, McKinley, Hayes, and Coolidge. Laurel Elizabeth Hicks tells readers of her *New World History and Geography in Christian Perspective*,[64] "William McKinley, the President of the United States, was a devout Christian who attended the Methodist church regularly. He took a courageous stand against liquor, swearing, and the telling of dirty stories, and he was known for his personal purity."[65]

The literature books developed by the two primary publishers for fundamentalist schools have a decidedly negative view toward writers, American and British. With few exceptions, the most prominent authors in both heritages are roundly accused of despair, pessimism, and religious apostasy. The writers are routinely judged not by established literary criteria but by their adherence or nonadherence to conservative Protestant values.

The selection of essays, short stories, poems, novels, and plays is skewed toward pious, didactic writings and frequently to mediocre writers deemed religiously safe. There is a clear preference for Protestant writers, especially those of the Puritan and Victorian eras. Major Catholic writers are either excluded, or their contributions are minimized. Extravagant and nonscholarly assertions and generalizations abound in the texts.

As this study makes clear, the views and attitudes expressed in these textbooks are sharply at variance with the major tenets of American democracy: respect for diversity, intellectual freedom, religious tolerance, racial and cultural pluralism, appreciation for modernity, experimentation, and pragmatism. All of these values are denied. Most are ridiculed. The fundamental concepts of the American democratic experiment are denounced repeatedly. Religious bigotry permeates these supposedly secular subject textbooks.[66]

Vouchers would compel all Americans to subsidize such instruction.

Notes

1. Rachel C. Larson with Pamela Creason, *The American Republic for Christian Schools* (Greenville, S.C.: Bob Jones University Press, 1988).

2. Ibid., p. 611.

3. Raymond A. St. John, *American Literature for Christian Schools, Book 1 (Early American Literature and American Romanticism)*, Teacher's Edition (Greenville, S.C.: Bob Jones University Press, 1991).

4. Ibid., p. 41.

5. Larson and Creason, *The American Republic for Christian Schools*, p. 447.

6. St. John, *American Literature for Christian Schools*, p. 542.

7. Larson and Creason, *The American Republic for Christian Schools*, p. 446.

8. Michael R. Lowman, *United States History in Christian Perspective* (Pensacola, Fla.: Pensacola Christian College, 1983).

9. Ibid., p. 221.

10. Larson and Creason, *The American Republic for Christian Schools*, p. 276.

11. Ibid., p. 62.

12. David A. Fisher, *World History for Christian Schools* (Greenville, S.C.: Bob Jones University Press, 1984), p. 130.

13. Ibid., p. 135.

14. Ronald A. Horton, *British Literature for Christian Schools: The Modern Tradition, 1688 to the Present* (Greenville, S.C.: Bob Jones University Press, 1982).

15. Ibid., p. 368.

16. Fisher, *World History for Christian Schools*, pp. 109–10.

17. Ibid., p. 116.

18. Ibid., p. 185.

19. Ibid., p. 203.

20. Glen Chambers and Gene Fisher, *United States History for Christian Schools* (Greenville, S.C.: Bob Jones University Press, 1982), p. 15.

21. Ibid., p. 92.

22. Ibid., p. 284.

23. Ibid., p. 349.

24. Ibid.

25. Ibid.

26. Lowman, *United States History in Christian Perspective*, p. 468.

27. Chambers and Fisher, *United States History for Christian Schools*, p. 15.

28. William S. Pinkston, Jr., *Biology for Christian Schools, Book 1*, Teacher's Edition (Greenville, S.C.: Bob Jones University Press, 1991), p. vii.

29. Ibid.

30. Ibid.

31. Ibid., p. 3.

32. Ibid., p. 25.

33. Ibid., p. 16.

34. Ibid., p. 25.

35. Ibid., p. 28.

36. Ibid., p. 172.

37. Ibid.

38. Ibid., p. 191.

39. William S. Pinkston, Jr., *Biology for Christian Schools, Book 2*, Teacher's Edition (Greenville, S.C.: Bob Jones University Press, 1991), p. 612.

40. Ibid., p. 491.

41. Ibid., p. 616.

42. Ibid., p. 643.

43. Ibid., p. 645.

44. Ibid.

45. Ibid., p. 639.

46. Ibid., p. 641.

47. Ibid., p. 640.

48. Chambers and Fisher, *United States History for Christian Schools*, p. 330.

49. Lowman, *United States History in Christian Perspective*, p. 471.

50. St. John, *American Literature for Christian Schools, Book 1,* p. 145.

51. Chambers and Fisher, *United States History for Christian Schools,* p. 80.

52. Ibid., pp. 564, 574, 575.

53. Ibid., pp. 563, 565, 574.

54. Ibid., p. 236.

55. Ibid., pp. 76–77.

56. Larson and Creason, *The American Republic for Christian Schools,* p. 420.

57. Fisher, *World History for Christian Schools,* pp. 548–49.

58. Larson and Creason, *The American Republic for Christian Schools,* p. 516.

59. Chambers and Fisher, *United States History for Christian Schools,* p. 550.

60. Ibid., p. 569.

61. Ibid., p. 577.

62. Lowman, *United States History in Christian Perspective,* p. 492.

63. Chambers and Fisher, *United States History for Christian Schools,* p. 332.

64. Laurel Elizabeth Hicks, *New World History and Geography in Christian Perspective* (Pensacola, Fla.: Pensacola Christian College, 1982).

65. Ibid., pp. 304–305.

66. For a more extensive treatment of this subject see Albert J. Menendez, *Visions of Reality: What Fundamentalist Schools Teach* (Amherst, N.Y.: Prometheus Books, 1993).

6

Vouchers and School Costs

Figuring the costs of various voucher plans can be tricky. An "experimental" voucher plan defeated by the U.S. Senate in July of 1994 had a one year price tag of $30 million, a relatively modest amount. But voucher plans defeated in state legislatures, such as in Pennsylvania, have had annual price tags in the hundreds of millions of dollars. Legislative attempts to get public funding for nonpublic schools usually aim to start modestly, for obvious political reasons. It's a matter of getting a foot in the door, or the camel's nose under the tent.

But the often-stated goal of promoters of voucher and other plans to get tax support for nonpublic schools is to achieve something close to per-student parity with tax support of public schools. Since there are about 4.9 million students in nonpublic schools, and since the average expenditure per year per public school student is around $5,500, more or less equal tax support of nonpublic schools could cost as much as $26.95 billion per year.

(Since public education is funded almost entirely from state and local taxes, and promoters of voucher plans are interested in both federal and state funding for nonpublic schools, there is an enormous potential for confusion and the creation of jurisdictional, economic, and administrative nightmares.)

In addition to the direct costs of voucher plans, we need to look at the unavoidable question of school transportation.

Implementing a voucher plan would not only require additional public expense for tuition costs, but also a great increase in transportation costs borne by state and local taxpayers. While the term "school choice" has an appealing ring, getting a student to a school, public or private, other than the public school in the student's own regular-attendance area will almost always require greatly increased transportation costs.

More than 57 percent of all public elementary and secondary school students were transported to school during the 1990–91 school year, at a total cost of over $9 billion.[1] According to the 1992 Carnegie Foundation report, 47 percent of public school students lived less than two miles from school (many who live within walking distance are bussed for safety reasons), 27 percent lived from two to five miles from school, 16 percent lived five to ten miles away, and 10 percent lived more than ten miles away.[2]

If a voucher or other "choice" plan were implemented and confined only to public schools, transportation costs would increase.

When the Carnegie Foundation surveyed parents in 1992 and asked, "Approximately how far is it to the next closest public school with your child's grade level?" one quarter of the parents responded less than two miles, another quarter two to five miles, a third quarter five to ten miles, and the remaining quarter ten miles or more.[3]

A voucher or other "choice" plan that allowed for open enrollment, even in other public school districts, or for attendance at nonpublic schools would escalate transportation costs astronomically, especially since the many different sorts of nonpublic schools would necessarily serve widely scattered constituencies.

Tax-paid transportation services for nonpublic schools are presently provided in twenty-seven states, states enrolling about 60 percent of nonpublic students. In those states per capita nonpublic school transportation costs already exceed public school costs by a considerable margin.[4] Implementation of a voucher plan would surely increase those costs and present problems for the twenty-three states that do not presently provide that service to nonpublic schools. School choice would often be meaningless if transportation services were not provided.

The Carnegie Foundation found that "transportation costs are especially important. Since parents in the same neighborhood may send their children to different schools, traditional bus routes will no longer work. As a result, many districts with "choice" programs have had to expand bus routes, run double shifts, or even hire fleets of taxis. In Kansas City, Missouri, which has a modified program, the district uses up to four hundred taxicabs to transport students from home to school."[5]

The Carnegie Foundation also reported:

> In Montclair [N.J.], transportation expenditures have
> increased by approximately $1.5 million annually as a
> result of the "choice" program. In Cambridge [MA], 15
> percent of the students rode school buses in 1981—the
> year before school choice was introduced. Now, 64 per-
> cent ride buses to get to school. As a result, transporta-
> tion costs in that district rose from $183,000 in 1981–82
> to $407,000 a decade later. Much of this increase
> reflected the added commitments imposed by choice.
> In St. Paul, school officials estimate that the average
> annual cost of transporting students who attend neigh-
> borhood schools is $120 per student. For students
> attending non-neighborhood "choice" schools, the
> average cost nearly triples, to $350.[6]

The Bush Education Department admitted that
"transportation also can be a limiting factor. It is costly
and complicated, and some 'choice' programs [in public
schools] have had to compromise on what would be the
most desirable system in order to stay within financial lim-
its or a reasonable travel distance."[7] Would this mean that
a voucher plan would have to favor some private schools
over others?

Tuition vouchers, then, would entail increasing costs
for transportation, costs that will have to be borne either
by taxpayers at the local and state levels or by parents, and
poorer parents are not likely to be able to cover those
costs.

The preceding deals only with the dollar costs of
voucher plans. Far beyond ready calculation are the
social costs of using public funds to divide our country's
children along religious, ideological, social class, ethnic,
and other lines. Equally beyond easy reckoning would be

the costs of replacing pluralistic democratic education with narrow forms of indoctrination.

Notes

1. Kern Alexander and Richard G. Salmon, *Public School Finance* (Boston: Allyn and Bacon, 1995), p. 221.

2. The Carnegie Foundation for the Advancement of Teaching, *School Choice* (Princeton, N.J.: 1992), p. 91.

3. Ibid., p. 16.

4. Edd Doerr and Albert J. Menendez, *Church Schools and Public Money* (Amherst, N.Y.: Prometheus Books, 1991), pp. 60–62.

5. Carnegie Foundation, *School Choice,* pp. 24–25.

6. Ibid., p. 24.

7. Office of Educational Research and Improvement (OERI), U.S. Department of Education, *Getting Started: How Choice Can Renew Your Public Schools* (Washington, D.C.: U.S. Government Printing Office, Aug. 1992), p. 26.

7

Public Education:
Myth and Reality

Public education is one of the cornerstones of American democracy and of the American way of life. It is accountable to those whose taxes finance it, and it reflects, albeit imperfectly, the values that have sustained and ennobled this republic for generations. That is why adoption of programs that threaten public education should be rejected.

Public education's performance varies widely from region to region, state to state, school district to school district, and even within districts. Funding of programs, the commitment of local political leaders, and economic and demographic realities all impact on the quality of public educational programs. Because public education serves a much wider and broader universe than the more selective non-public schools, the public sector's performance is really quite remarkable. Two recent studies have demonstrated this.

A ground-breaking study by *Money* magazine in October 1994 concludes that Americans who pay high tuitions for private school tuition are "probably wasting their hard-earned money." The nationally respected monthly also concluded that:

- Students who attend the best public schools outperform most private school students.

- The average public school teacher has stronger academic qualifications than the average private school teacher.

- The best public schools offer a more challenging curriculum than most private schools.

- Public school class sizes are no larger than in most private schools and are smaller than in most Catholic schools.

These conclusions startled *Money*'s editors, who admitted that many send their children to expensive private schools, blithely assuming that their superiority was demonstrable and unshakable. The editors selected ten typical schools in seven categories: Public schools that serve advantaged pupils, average-income students, and disadvantaged neighborhoods; nonsectarian prep schools that "historically have educated the nation's elite"; religious prep schools, usually Catholic, Episcopalian or Quaker; Roman Catholic parish or diocesan schools; and other parochial schools serving Protestant and other non-Catholic communities. Nineteen *Money* reporters and correspondents visited the schools, and, in some instances, administrators were interviewed by phone. It was an ambitious and thorough survey, supported in part by School Match, a Westerville, Ohio, firm that helps parents select the "right" schools for their children.

The survey probed the variables of selectivity and income, which affect school performance across the board. Challenging the use of test scores as the only criterion by which school performance is judged, *Money* observed, "It is true that test scores are higher at private and parochial schools than they are at public schools. But the explanation is not the quality of education the schools offer. Rather, it is a consequence of their varying selectivity. Public schools are legally obligated to educate all children who live within their districts, while prep schools have the luxury of rejecting two of every three applicants."

Private schools clearly serve a more affluent clientele. While only 11 percent of all U.S. students attend private schools, fully 30 percent of students living in affluent neighborhoods attend nonpublic schools.

Catholic schools slightly outperform public schools which serve middle or lower income students, but most experts consulted by *Money* concluded "that the differences would vanish if researchers could control the fact that Catholic schools can pick and choose their students. . . . While not as selective as the elite prep schools, the Catholic schools we looked at rejected as many as two-thirds of all applicants." Interestingly, "Catholic schools were less successful in sending their graduates to four-year colleges" than non-Catholic parochial schools, the report found.

Teacher quality is higher and curricula more varied in public schools, according to *Money* reporters. "According to the National Center for Education Statistics, half of all public school teachers hold advanced degrees, vs. only a third of private school instructors." The least well-educated instructors are those who teach at Protestant schools. Public school teachers also have more experience, since 67 percent have taught for a decade or more, compared to 42 percent in private academies and 55 percent in Catholic schools.

Money concluded that "top public schools offer as many challenging courses as prep schools do" and "public schools offer arts and sports programs that often exceed those found at private schools."

Public schools serving advantaged students also have good learning environments, quality facilities, and few discipline problems.

Admittedly, the least academically successful public schools were those which served poor neighborhoods. Disadvantaged students still receive inferior educations, a scandal that this society can no longer afford.

The distinguished Carnegie Foundation for the Advancement of Teaching issued an important report in 1992 on *School Choice*, which concludes that there is little substantive proof that the much-heralded choice or voucher plans to alter the education enterprise in America will really do the job their promoters claim. Tax-subsidized vouchers, which could be used in private and parochial as well as public schools, will not improve the quality of education or the availability of options and alternatives to the disadvantaged.

The authors of this excellent report have studied existing choice plans in various states and cities and found them wanting in many respects. The Carnegie researchers surveyed all fifty state school officers to ascertain the present status of the "school choice" movement.

The researchers found that existing choice plans widened the gap between advantaged and disadvantaged school districts, often causing near bankruptcy in the poorest sectors. Transportation costs increase markedly. They also discerned that the choice movement stresses only the "private benefits" of schooling, not the "social imperatives of promoting the common good" which is essential to a just society. The report notes, "While reflecting on the current school-choice debate, we were impressed by just how little attention is being given to the history of public education or to the large body of thought about the role of schooling in building a democratic nation." Furthermore they say, "It's time to reaffirm public education and commit ourselves to having a school of quality within the reach of every child. . . . Instead of bashing schools, let's celebrate success and build on the good practices now in place."

The Carnegie report also reminds us that "the crises in education relate not just to school governance but to the pathologies that surround the schools."

The much-touted Milwaukee plan, a publicly-funded private school choice scheme, has not proved successful, according to Carnegie researchers. The attrition rate is high, and no discernible improvement in student test scores has been achieved. "Whatever else may be said of it, Milwaukee's plan has failed to demonstrate that vouchers can, in and of themselves, spark school improvement," the report concluded.

Ernest L. Boyer, president of the Carnegie Foundation, reminds us that "choice has moved to the top of the national agenda" and must be confronted on its merits. But the national debate must not ignore the profound impact that educational change will have on children, parents, teachers, and schools. Writes Boyer, "While some of our schools are outstanding, ranking among the best in the world, others are desperately disadvantaged. These schools are failing not from bureaucratic gridlock, but from pathologies that surround them—neglected children, troubled families, and neighborhoods in decay."

The Carnegie Foundation is right. Improving public education is a national necessity. Various schemes to divert funds to private-interest or church-based education must be resisted. Boyer has the last word: "We believe the public schools remain the best hope for strengthening our democratic nation."

The overall "condition" of American education is complex, but there are significant areas of progress and reasons for optimism. The annual report mandated by Congress, *The Condition of Education 1995,*[1] found that American public school students are scoring higher on mathematics and science proficiency, are dropping out of high school at a lower rate, and are continuing their education after graduation in greater numbers than in previous years.

The annual report, prepared by the National Center for Education Statistics, a division of the Department of Education, measures sixty indicators of the overall quality of United States education. Data on enrollment, student achievement, revenue and expenditures on schools, teacher salaries, and graduation rates are among the areas studied by educational researchers.

The report shows steady progress in meeting some of

the goals outlined in the landmark 1983 report, "A Nation at Risk." For example, the percentage of high school graduates who took geometry increased from 48 percent to 70 percent between 1982 and 1992, the last year for which information is available.[2] A similar increase occurred in chemistry, with 32 percent of graduates taking a chemistry course in 1982 and 56 percent doing so in 1992.[3] Mathematics and science proficiency scores also increased by 9 and 11 points respectively during the same period.[4]

During the measurable period covered by the 1995 study, the percentage of all high school students who took advanced math and science courses increased from 13 percent to 47 percent.[5]

More students enrolled in college immediately following high school graduation. The percentage rose from 49 percent in 1980 to 62 percent in 1993.[6] The percentage of students using a computer at home or at school rose from 35 percent to 68 percent.[7]

In comparison with other industrialized nations, the United States ranks first in the percentage of its citizens who graduate from college, and about even with Germany and Japan in the percentage of twenty-five to thirty-four-year-olds who complete high school. Teacher salaries have increased almost 21 percent since 1982,[8] and only 5 percent of teachers leave the profession annually, mostly to retire or raise children.[9]

The report indicated some real and seemingly intractable problems that the nation has yet to address, and which will continue to affect policymakers in the years to come. One of them is that reading and writing skills have not improved appreciably.

Many educational problems are related to poverty, disparity in educational funding, and to language problems. Nearly 22 percent of U.S. children are living in poverty— 46 percent of blacks, 39 percent of Hispanics, and 16 percent of whites. "The schools in these neighborhoods face heavy demands," says Emerson J. Elliott, Commissioner of Education Statistics, who added, "Violence in and around schools directly affects educators and students by reducing school effectiveness and inhibiting students' learning."[10]

Americans of Hispanic ancestry have fared the poorest educationally. Only 60 percent of Hispanic twenty-five to twenty-nine-year-olds had completed high school in 1994, compared to 84 percent of African-Americans and 91 percent of whites.[11]

Family income continues to affect all aspects of the educational experience. In 1993, for example, 79 percent of high school graduates from high income families went to college, compared to 57 percent of those in middle income families and 50 percent in low income families.[12]

We know also that academic performance and SAT scores are related to family income and resources:

> Statistics for 1991 from the Carnegie Foundation for the Advancement of Teaching show that SAT scores are directly proportional to family income. Students from families with incomes under $10,000 score an average of 788 (combined verbal and math scores) out of a possible 1200. Students from families with incomes in the $30,000-$40,000 range have scores averaging 884, and those whose family incomes are over $70,000 have averages of 997.[13]

As for the often-heard claim that nonpublic schools are superior to public schools:

> The National Assessment of Education Progress (NAEP) shows that the NAEP math scores are nearly identical when public and private school students of the same family backgrounds are compared. The apparent differences between public and private schools are a result of the selectivity of private schools. They serve proportionately only one-fourth as many children from families with incomes under $15,000 as public schools do, while enrolling proportionately more than three times as many pupils from families with incomes over $50,000.[14]

With all of its problems, American public education seems to be performing remarkably well.

Notes

1. National Center for Education Statistics, *The Condition of Education 1995* (Washington, D.C.: U.S. Department of Education, Office of Educational Research and Improvement, 1995), Document No. NCES 95–273.
2. Ibid., pp. 80–81.
3. Ibid.
4. Ibid., pp. 58–59.
5. Ibid., pp. 78–79.
6. Ibid., pp. 42–43.
7. Ibid., pp. 34–35.
8. Ibid., p. 158.
9. Ibid., p. 164.

10. Ibid., p. xi.

11. Ibid., p. 72.

12. Ibid., p. 42.

13. John M. Swomley, "The Illusion of Parental Choice," *The Human Quest* (September–October 1993): 9.

14. Ibid., p. 9.

8

Vouchers: Empty Promises

American public schools, like all institutions everywhere, could stand improvement. But while there is broad agreement among educators and parents that more adequate and more equitable funding for public schools is an essential ingredient in any effort to upgrade them, a budget-cutting mood in the country makes such funding problematic. However, one "reform" (with a deliberately concealed fiscal and social price tag) being advocated by some politicians, some economists, and some denominational special interests and pressure groups is getting a great deal of attention: vouchers. Various voucher plans, promoted under the beguiling banners of "market" and "parental choice," ignore the fact that most nonpublic schools interested in getting tax support through vouchers tend to select students using criteria not legally or socially acceptable in public schools.

Voucher advocates such as Chubb and Moe[1] criticize public schools for being responsible to elected boards and for having bureaucracies to carry out policies developed by those boards. Their arguments for vouchers and other "parental choice" plans have been carefully examined by two political scientists from the University of Nebraska and the University of Wisconsin, Kevin B. Smith and Kenneth J. Meier, in a recent well-documented book.[2] They conclude:

> Probably the most comprehensive studies of school choice done to date are those conducted by the U.S. Department of Education (1992), the Carnegie Foundation (1992), and political scientist Jeffrey Henig (1994). None corroborates the promised benefits of choice. The Carnegie Foundation report in particular found that although choice does indeed provide important benefits in specific cases, overall its impact is mixed. Among other things, this study reported that choice's effect on academic improvement was far from uniform, that participation in the existing programs is extremely low, and that choice can be a tremendously expensive reform to implement and sustain. Where choice has been implemented and studied in other countries, the results have been mixed or disappointing.[3]

Because nonpublic schools tend to be selective academically and in other ways, "cream-skimming" by nonpublic schools, whether aided by vouchers or not, tends to have a negative effect on public school performance.[4] "Cream-skimming," selecting or giving preference to the "best" students, could also occur in choice plans confined

to public schools and thus "exacerbate the already considerable inequities among school districts."[5]

> Two selection mechanisms . . . provide a student body
> for most private schools that is different from that of
> public schools. The market pricing system eliminates
> some students who would be difficult to educate, and
> the school's admissions procedures screen out the
> rest. . . .[6]
>
> Services based around religion, not quality, consti-
> tute a large reason for the demand for private school
> education.[7]
>
> The cream-skimming finding is equally devastating
> for the public choice model. It suggests that private
> school performance is a function of limiting inputs by
> restricting access to the best and most educable stu-
> dents. Schools find it fairly easy to educate white mid-
> dle-class students from stable families; it is much more
> difficult to educate poor, racially diverse students from
> broken families. Additional support for the cream-
> skimming hypotheses can be found in the Milwaukee
> school choice experiment. In that experiment, private
> schools cannot cream; if they agree to participate in
> the program, they must take all students assigned to
> them. In addition, only school-lunch-eligible students
> can participate in the choice program. As a result, the
> elite private schools in the Milwaukee area have
> refused to participate in the program. If they have to
> play on a level playing field, the private schools opt not
> to play. . . .[8]
>
> Embryonic school choice programs [confined to
> public schools] are not associated with any gains in
> performance—they are, in fact, associated with a loss.
> The reforms that school choice theorists argued to be

ineffective distractions of symbolic politics are instead associated with solid and significant gains in performance.[9]

It needs to be reiterated that use of the term "parental choice" in promoting voucher plans is largely a propaganda gimmick, since it is the private school that actually makes the choice. For example, draft legislation in Wisconsin is worded so that "a school affiliated with a religious organization may extend preferential treatment to students of the same religious affiliation or to siblings of those already enrolled." In plain English, the private school may discriminate along religious lines. Nothing would require schools to accept those with poor academic potential, or those with disciplinary records or other liabilities.[10]

Moreover, most of the available nonpublic schools are permeated with particular sectarian denominational teachings. Parents of a different religion than that of the school have no choice. They must either risk putting their children into a school that will try to convert them to a different faith, or forego the tax credit or voucher. This is hardly parental choice. It is governmental-dictated or induced choice.[11]

Aside from religious considerations, "parental choice" is further limited when private school curricula are devised to serve more limited constituencies. Schools that have stiff academic entrance requirements can hardly be chosen by students of limited ability. Schools that do not offer vocational education, home economics, or programs for children with handicaps do not by their very nature offer viable choices to many students. Schools that require classes in Hebrew or Arabic will rarely be chosen by non-Jewish or non-Muslim families. Amish schools will not be chosen by students planning to go on to study physics at MIT. Schools that require payment of tuition above the value of the tax-paid voucher can be chosen only by well-to-do families.

In the voucher debate, then, "parental choice" will quite often be little more than an empty slogan.

Albert Shanker, president of the American Federation of Teachers, writes that it is a mistake to think that using private school vouchers is equivalent to shopping at Macy's with a "big fat gift certificate." Using vouchers, Shanker says, is more analogous to applying for membership in an exclusive club.

> Private country clubs don't accept you merely because you have filled out an application form and you can pay the fees. A club that needs more warm bodies might be happy to get money on the barrel. But in an exclusive country club, the membership committee might ask itself how you fit in with the crowd that already belongs. And if they have any doubts, they'll probably decide that it's not worth the risk of losing a bunch of old members to get one new member. You can choose a country club, but the real choice is the club's.[12]

Voucher plan proponents often assert that vouchers will somehow improve public education by creating competition. National PTA's Arnold Fege responds:

> The "healthy rivalry" between the public and private schools envisioned with the introduction of a voucher

program is really an unfair match in which one com-
petitor—the private school—does not have to play by
the same rules as the public schools. Many public
schools and those receiving federal monies must
adhere to:

Title VI of the Civil Rights Act of 1964, which protects students against discrimination on the basis of
race, color, or national origin.

Title IX of the Education Amendments of 1972,
which protects the rights of women and girls in educational programs or activities.

Section 504 of the Rehabilitation Act of 1971,
which prohibits schools from discriminating against
disabled persons.

The Age Discrimination Act of 1975, which prohibits discrimination on the basis of age.

In addition, many states and local communities
have created public policies related to safety, curriculum, teacher certification, and environmental protec-
tions for public schools. With the exception of race,
nonpublic schools receiving vouchers do not have to
abide by these regulations, especially if they do not
receive federal dollars. Vouchers then become a vehi-
cle that allows circumvention of laws and regulations
designed to meet the common needs of children, parents, the community, and the nation. Private schools
are then able to pick and choose those regulations and
policies that they wish to follow. For instance, if a private school does not wish to educate handicapped children because the cost is too great, they do not have to
admit them. If a religious school wishes to admit students only of their own faith, they may. If a private
school wishes to exclude women from their sports program, they may. This unfair framework of "competi-

tion" would have the effect of creating a dual school system: a public one that would be required to meet the common needs of a community and nation, and a private one that would be exempt from many of the regulations in order to accommodate the special requirements of its children and their parents.[13]

Further, regarding the idea that privatization will lead to excellence, Fege writes:

Voucher proponents assume a cause-effect relationship between competition and quality in the marketplace and that a similar dynamic would work with schools. In business, however, the relationship between competition and quality is a function of profit. If a company can show greater profit by providing a cheaper, lower-quality product or no-frills service, it will. If a service— e.g., hospitalization for the poor or airline service to smaller communities—is not profitable, it won't be provided. A company is not in business to give the consumer the best product or service at the lowest price but to improve its profit margin by any method that will work. Competition, then, impacts pricing far more than it does product quality.[14]

Fege also challenges the claim that a private school voucher program would promote quality in all schools:

It is difficult to understand the logic of this conclusion. First, upon the inception of a private school voucher program, the children already in private schools would receive vouchers. This would have no effect in improving any schools because the parents have already made their selection *without* the incentive of a voucher.

Second, the cost of each voucher would be skimmed off the top of the respective public education budget, local and/or state, and funneled to the private schools. This financial drain would be at the expense of the public schools, many of which are already experiencing funding shortages and a "no new taxes" environment. For instance, the average per-student expenditure for each elementary and secondary school student in the United States in 1990 was approximately $4,200. In a state that had 50,000 nonpublic school students and that provided a voucher to each of those students at, shall we say, $2,100, or half of the per-student average, it would reduce public school funds by approximately $105 million unless the taxpayers decided to increase revenues. It is inconceivable how such a program would enable the public schools to improve. In fact, vouchers would have the effect of giving private schools a distinct advantage by redistributing existing education dollars in favor of nonpublic schools without any assurances that education will improve for *all* children.

Third, a 1991 report released by the Committee for Economic Development, an independent research and educational organization comprising over 250 business and education leaders, concluded that· "new research into student achievement demonstrates that, by itself, choice does not guarantee educational quality. . . . We believe that where choice systems are put into place, they should involve the public schools only."[15]

Notes

1. John E. Chubb and Terry Moe, *Politics, Markets, and America's Schools* (Washington, D.C.: Brookings Institution, 1990).

2. Kevin B. Smith and Kenneth J. Meier, *The Case Against School Choice* (Armonk, N.Y.: M. E. Sharpe, 1995).

3. Ibid., p. 26.

4. Ibid., p. 49.

5. Ibid., p. 61.

6. Ibid., p. 65.

7. Ibid., p. 66.

8. Ibid., p. 77.

9. Ibid., p. 104.

10. John M. Swomley, "Parental Choice and Tuition Tax Credits," *Christian Social Action* (September 1993): 14.

11. Ibid.

12. Quoted in Arnold F. Fege, "Private School Vouchers: Separate and Unequal," in *Why We Still Need Public Schools*, ed. Art Must, Jr. (Amherst, N.Y.: Prometheus Books, 1992), p. 229.

13. Ibid., pp. 225–26

14. Ibid., pp. 228–29.

15. Ibid., pp. 226–27.

Appendix A

Milwaukee's Voucher "Experiment"

On August 25, 1995, the Wisconsin Supreme Court issued a preliminary injunction halting the expansion of Milwaukee's voucher "experiment" to include denominational private schools.[1] A hearing on a permanent injunction is to be held in the fall of 1995. The ruling came in a suit filed by the American Civil Liberties Union on behalf of a group of Milwaukee parents and religious leaders. The injunction was praised by Milwaukee school board president Mary Bills, who said, "It was the right decision for the children and their families and the Milwaukee public school system."

Milwaukee's voucher "experiment" began five years earlier, largely at the instigation of Gov. Tommy G. Thompson. Until 1995 the plan had been confined to low-income students in Milwaukee and to nonsectarian private schools. During the 1994-95 school year only about 830 students were enrolled in the program, though there were 1,450 places available. Only twelve of the city's twenty-three nonreligious private schools chose to be involved in the plan.

Kevin Keane, a spokesman for Gov. Thompson, said that as of August 25 about 3,500 vouchers had been issued for the coming school year since the voucher plan was changed by the legislature earlier in the year to allow religious private schools to participate. Had the state's high court not enjoined the participation of the religious schools, the Milwaukee school district stood to lose about $7 million in state funds, which school board president Bills said would have forced the public schools to cut back on programs and/or services.

Under the Milwaukee voucher plan students receive vouchers worth up to $3,600, which are to be redeemed for cash by the participating private schools.

Even before the state supreme court ruling, the Milwaukee program was running into problems, according to a report in the *Milwaukee Journal Sentinel.*[2] A number of parents complained that their children were being illegally screened out on the basis of previous school performance. Other parents complained of children being kept out by registration fees of $50 to $350 and by tuition and uniform fees. Under the Wisconsin voucher law participating students are supposed to be able to attend the private schools without charge.

While voucher advocates have touted the Milwaukee program as an important demonstration project, the actual results are not impressive. The Carnegie Foundation study reported:

Thus far the evidence from that city is not encouraging. While most students and parents participating in the program say they are happy with their chosen schools, an astonishing 40 percent of students who made the switch to private schools did not return the next year. Further, the standard test scores of participating students have shown little or no improvement in reading and math and remain well below average in both. . . .

The Milwaukee experiment also demonstrates the hazards of introducing private school choice without providing for public accountability. Proponents of choice argue that to impose state oversight on private schools would force them into the same mold that has restricted the creativity of public education. The argument seems appealing. Yet in the first years of Milwaukee's plan, one school shut down in a cloud of scandal, and the performance standards met by most of the remaining schools were marginal, at best.[3]

Another problem with the Milwaukee plan is that, unlike public schools, the participating private schools have the option of rejecting handicapped children. In 1990 U.S. Undersecretary of Education Ted Sanders issued an opinion to the effect that the participating private schools would not be required to comply with the federal Education for All Handicapped Children Law.[4] This highlights an important difference between public and nonpublic schools. Handicapped students, who require much more expensive education than the non-handicapped, make up only 1.5 percent of nonpublic enrollment but 4.9 percent of public school enrollment.[5]

The Carnegie study also found flaws in the commonly

reported claim that private schools can educate children for about half of what is spent per student in public schools. First of all, their costs are lowered by their being able to keep out handicapped children. Then, the Milwaukee plan's original $2,600 voucher did not cover the true cost of $3,000 to $3,500 (compared to $5,000 per student spent in public schools). Some of the participating Milwaukee private schools resorted to requiring parents to engage in fund-raising and volunteer work. Participating private schools also received some private foundation support, and kept costs down by paying teachers only about half the salaries of Milwaukee public school teachers and providing fewer benefits to teachers.[6]

It is clear that if nonpublic schools paid their teachers the same as public school teachers, accepted handicapped children as public schools must and do, and provided the same level and variety of educational services as public schools, their per-student costs would be just as high as those of public schools. They would probably be higher because private schools are generally smaller and thus less efficient and cost-effective than public schools.

Notes

1. Kimberly J. McLarin, "Court Bars Voucher Plan in Religious Schools," *New York Times*, August 26, 1995.

2. Curtis Lawrence, "Some in Wisconsin Say Fees, Grades Hinder School Choice," reprinted in *The Washington Times*, August 23, 1995.

3. The Carnegie Foundation, *School Choice* (Princeton, N.J.: 1992), pp. 17-19.

4. Ibid., p. 68.

5. Smith and Meier, *The Case against School Choice* (Armonk, N.J.: M. E. Sharpe, 1995), p. 78.

6. Carnegie Foundation, *School Choice,* p. 71.

Appendix B

Nonpublic School Enrollment by State

One of the more objectionable features of proposed voucher plans is that they will transfer funds from some states to others, in addition to redistributing public school money to private and religious schools. The following information comes from a report prepared in June 1994 by the U.S. Department of Education's National Center for Education Statistics. Called "Private School Survey, 1991-92," it gives the enrollment of private elementary and secondary schools by state for the fall of 1991. At that time 4,889,545 students were enrolled in nonpublic schools. Of these, 53.0 percent attended Catholic schools, 32.2 percent attended other religious schools, and 14.8 percent were enrolled in nonsectarian schools.

115

Percent of Students Attending Private Schools

Rank	State	Percentage	Rank	State	Percentage
1	Delaware	18.2	26	Alabama	8.8
2	Hawaii	18.0	27	Colorado	8.8
3	Pennsylvania	17.5	28	Vermont	7.9
4	New Jersey	15.9	29	Georgia	7.6
5	New York	15.9	30	South Dakota	7.4
6	Louisiana	14.9	31	Virginia	7.4
7	Wisconsin	14.9	32	Kansas	7.3
8	Illinois	14.0	33	New Mexico	7.2
9	Ohio	13.9	34	Washington	7.1
10	Maryland	13.4	35	South Carolina	6.8
11	Rhode Island	13.0	36	Maine	6.4
12	Massachusetts	12.9	37	North Dakota	6.0
13	Nebraska	12.4	38	Montana	5.8
14	Connecticut	12.3	39	Oregon	5.8
15	Missouri	12.3	40	Arizona	5.7
16	Minnesota	10.8	41	North Carolina	5.4
17	California	10.7	42	Oklahoma	5.4
18	Michigan	10.5	43	Arkansas	4.9
19	Mississippi	10.4	44	Texas	4.7
20	Florida	9.6	45	Alaska	4.4
21	New Hampshire	9.6	46	Nevada	3.9
22	Iowa	9.5	47	West Virginia	3.9
23	Indiana	9.4	48	Idaho	2.9
24	Kentucky	9.3	49	Utah	2.1
25	Tennessee	9.1	50	Wyoming	1.8

Appendix C

What Others Have Said

Justice William J. Brennan

It is implicit in the history and character of American public education that the public schools serve a uniquely public function: the training of American citizens in an atmosphere free of parochial, divisive, or separatist influence of any sort—an atmosphere in which children may assimilate a heritage common to all American groups and religions.

Concurring Opinion,
Abington School District v. *Schempp*
374 U.S. 241, 242.

Michael Casserly,
Executive Director
Council of the Great City Schools

Public education is being challenged now once again, not just to move with the nation's emerging sense of its own democracy and opportunity, but to address ever greater challenges of both global competition and domestic turmoil. Unfortunately, many now view the country's educational system as not up to the task of getting us where we need to go to meet our immediate challenges. Ironically, the solution being espoused by some is to revert to the kind of elite and privatized system that the nation rejected as insufficient years ago. . . .

Public schools continue to be the only national mechanism through which our country's common values are articulated and disseminated, even in our polyglot environment.

"Why Public Schools?" in
Art Must, Jr., *Why We Still Need Public Schools*
(Amherst, N.Y.: Prometheus Books, 1992)

Monsignor Thomas J. Curry

There is simply no possibility that Catholic education can receive substantial public assistance and that the church can at the same time maintain complete control and direction of its schools. The reception of public monies must inevitably involve public supervision or control. . . .

The greatest danger for Catholic schools is not that they may fail to secure public assistance, but that in order to receive such aid they may secularize themselves piecemeal in the process.

America, April 5, 1986.

Senator Sam J. Ervin, Jr.

Government is contemptuous of true religion when it confiscates the taxes of Caesar to finance the things of God.

"Open Letter to President Reagan,"
Congressional Record, April 29, 1982.

Arnold F. Fege,
Director of Governmental Relations
National PTA

There are fundamental flaws in private and religious school voucher proposals. By diverting attention and resources away from the public schools, the controversial voucher movement may have the effect of dismantling public education rather than strengthening it. There is also the possibility that private schools will lose the freedoms they have due to encroaching government regulations as a trade-off for receiving public dollars.

"Private School Vouchers: Separate and Unequal"
in Art Must, Jr., *Why We Still Need Public Schools*
(Amherst, N.Y.: Prometheus Books, 1992).

Florence Flast, Vice-Chair
Committee for Public Education
and Religious Liberty (PEARL)

Religious liberty in America means not only the right to pursue one's own beliefs, but freedom from compulsory taxation to foster the religious beliefs of others. . . .

A proliferation of state-financed private and religious schools would greatly increase the tax burden on our citizenry. It would encourage racial, class and religious segregation, pitting one group against another in the political arena in bitter competition for the tax dollar. It would invite religious conflicts and the inequities of Southern style school segregation. . . .

The survival of free public education, the integrity of religious institutions, and the security of American democracy all demand an end to government financing of sectarian schools.

> "Why Parochiaid is a Threat to
> Public Education and Religious Liberty,"
> statement issued June 12, 1972.

The Fleischmann Report

Civic tranquility is best maintained by having the state remain apart from the sphere of religion and religious institutions.

> New York, 1972.

Benjamin Franklin

When a religion is good, I conceive it will support itself; and when it does not support itself, and God does not take care to support it so that its professors are obliged to call for help of the civil power, 'tis a sign, I apprehend, of its being a bad one.

> Anson Phelps Stokes, *Church and State in the United States* (New York: Harper, 1950), 1:298.

President James Garfield

Next in importance to freedom and justice is popular education, without which neither justice nor freedom can be permanently maintained. Its interests are intrusted to the States and the voluntary action of the people. Whatever help the nation can justly afford should be generously given to aid the States in supporting common schools; but it would be unjust to our people and dangerous to our institutions to apply any portion of the revenues of the nation or of the States to the support of sectarian schools. The separation of Church and State in everything relating to taxation should be absolute.

> Letter of acceptance of presidential nomination, July 12, 1880.

Joanne Goldsmith, Executive Director National Coalition for Public Education and Religious Liberty (PEARL)

The great majority of Americans firmly oppose the use of government funds to help finance religiously affiliated schools. . . . We hope that Congress will recognize that proposals for federal aid to sectarian schools embody a substantial and harmful departure from constitutional principle and tradition.

Testimony, U.S. House of Representatives,
September 21, 1977.

President Ulysses S. Grant

Encourage free schools and resolve that not one dollar appropriated for their support shall be appropriated to the support of any sectarian schools. Resolve that neither the state nor nation, nor both combined, shall support institutions of learning other than those sufficient to afford every child growing up in the land of opportunity of a good common school education, unmixed with sectarian, pagan, or atheistical dogmas. Leave the matter of religion to the family altar, the church and the private school supported entirely by private contributions. Keep the church and state forever separate.

Address to the Army of the Tennessee,
Des Moines, Iowa, September 25, 1875.

Herbert Grover, Superintendent of Public Instruction, Wisconsin

Julie K. Underwood, Professor, University of Wisconsin

A private school voucher program encourages the abandonment of the social institution best able and most likely to preserve our commitment to equal opportunity, pluralism, and cultural diversity. Without a societal commitment to the institution of public education, the tendency would be for people to flee one another in search of their own isolated educational repose, returning to pre-1954 when separate passed for equal.

"The Milwaukee Parental Choice Program" in Art Must, Jr., *Why We Still Need Public Schools* (Amherst, N.Y.: Prometheus Books, 1992).

President John F. Kennedy

I believe in an America where the separation of church and state is absolute—where no Catholic prelate would tell the President (should he be Catholic) how to act and no Protestant minister would tell his parishioners for whom to vote—where no church or church school is granted any public funds or political preference— and where no man is denied public office merely because his religion differs from the President who might appoint him or the people who might elect him.

Address to the Ministerial Association of Greater Houston, September 12, 1960.

Michael Lind

The conservative plan to replace public schools with taxpayer subsidized vouchers to private schools would reinforce the growing segregation of America by class. If vouchers were not linked to government caps on tuition, expensive private schools would simply raise their tuitions by the amount of the voucher, to continue pricing out all but the wealthiest students. Even worse, middle-class American parents would find themselves being taxed to pay for the vouchers of rich children attending schools from which middle-class children could be legally turned away because their parents did not make enough money.

The Next American Nation: The New Nationalism
and the Fourth American Revolution
(New York: The Free Press, 1995), p. 213.

The Living Church
Episcopal magazine

Christians who care enough about their faith to want it properly taught to their children in the course of their education should care enough to pay for it, however heavy the burden. . . . When any of our tax money is used, directly or indirectly, to subsidize any religious teaching without our consent, government is coercing us in this realm where coercion does not belong.

Editorial, April 21, 1974.

Miami Herald

For good reason that has nothing to do with religious prejudice, the nation decided long ago that public funds should not be diverted to private schools.

Editorial, October 16, 1972.

National Education Association

The National Education Association believes that voucher plans or funding formulas that have the same effect as vouchers—under which education is financed by federal, state, or local grants to parents, schools, or school systems—could lead to racial, economic, and social isolation of students and weaken or destroy the public school system.

NEA Handbook, 1994-1995
(Washington, D.C., 1994), p. 248.

The New York Times

We respect the right of parents to send their children to religious schools if they wish, but they should recognize that this is a voluntary choice on their part. The state has no obligation to further religious training in this way. In fact, it has an obligation to keep hands off

Editorial, M

G. Bromley Oxnam
Methodist Bishop

If parents have the natural right to determine the education of their children, a privilege this nation gladly gives, it follows that parents who refuse the benefits of these splendid public educational opportunities should pay for such private education as they insist upon.

The Nation's Schools (March, 1947).

President Theodore Roosevelt

Because we are unqualifiedly and without reservation against any system of denominational schools, maintained by the adherents of any creed with the help of state aid, therefore, we as strenuously insist that the public schools shall be free from sectarian influences, and above all, free from any attitude of hostility to the adherents of any particular creed.

Quoted in Reuben Maury, *The Wars of the Godly* (New York, 1928), p. 213.

I hold that in this country there must be complete severance of Church and State; that public moneys shall not be used for the purpose of advancing any particular creed; and therefore that the public schools shall be nonsectarian and no public moneys appropriated for sectarian schools.

Address, Carnegie Hall, October 12, 1915.

Elihu Root
U.S. Secretary of State
under Theodore Roosevelt

It is not a question of religion, or of creed, or of party; it is a question of declaring and maintaining the great American principle of eternal separation between Church and State.

Statement Against the Use of Public Funds for Sectarian Education by the State of New York, 1894.

Alfred E. Smith
Governor of New York
Democratic candidate for President, 1928

I believe in the support of the public school as one of the cornerstones of American liberty. I believe in the right of every parent to choose whether his child shall be educated in the public school or in a religious school supported by those of his own faith.

Atlantic Monthly, April 1927.

Unitarian Universalist Association

WHEREAS, the constitutional principles of religious liberty and the separation of church and state that safeguards liberty, and the ideal of a pluralistic society are under increasing attack in the Congress of the United States, in state legislatures, and in some sectors of the communications media by a combination of sectarian and secular special interests;

BE IT RESOLVED: That the 1982 General Assembly of UUA reaffirms its support for these principles and urges the Board of Trustees and President of the Association, member societies, and Unitarian Universalists in the United States to:

1. Defend the democratic, pluralistic public school, opposing all forms of direct and indirect public aid to support sectarian private schools, such as tuition tax credits or vouchers. . . .

General Assembly Resolution, Approved 1982.

United Methodist Church

We believe in the principle of universal public education, and we reaffirm our support of public educational institutions. At the same time, we recognize and pledge our continued allegiance to the U.S. Constitutional principle that citizens have a right to establish and maintain private schools from private resources so long as such schools meet public standards of quality. Such schools have made a genuine contribution to society. We do not support the expansion or the strengthening of private schools with public funds. Furthermore, we oppose the establishment or strengthening of private schools that jeopardize the public school system or thwart valid public policy.

We specifically oppose tuition tax credits or any other mechanism which directly or indirectly allows government funds to support religious schools at the primary and secondary level. Persons of one particular faith should be free to use their own funds to strengthen the belief system of their particular religious group. But they should not expect all taxpayers, including those who adhere to other religious belief systems, to provide funds to teach religious views with which they do not agree. . . .

Finally, churches should not seek to utilize the processes of public affairs to further their own institutional interests or to obtain special privileges for themselves.

Excerpts from General Assembly Resolution, 1980.
(Operative language reaffirmed 1992.)

Washington Post

Public schools, controlled by public boards of education maintained by public funds and open to all the public regardless of race or religion, have served this country magnificently well. They have been usefully supplemented by private schools, privately controlled and maintained, offering special forms of education and indoctrination to pupils with special needs and desires. It would be a misfortune to confuse the two, especially where religion is concerned. For a separation of church from state has been proved by history to be an indispensable condition alike for political liberty and for religious liberty. Let religious teaching remain within the province of homes and churches and private schools. Let secular education remain within the province of governments controlled by the people and open to all the winds of politics.

Editorial, June 21, 1969.

Americans have every right, of course, to seek for their children a religiously oriented education and to send their children to private schools which provide the sort of religious orientation they want. But they have no more right to ask the general public to pay for such schools—and for the religious instruction they provide—than to ask the general public to pay for the churches in which, happily, they are free to gather for prayer and for worship as they please.

The religious schools are organs of a church. The public schools are organs of a secular authority, the state. Would it not be wiser, as the founders of the Republic concluded, to keep church and state altogether separate?

Editorial, March 3, 1971.

Board of Education v. *Allen* (1968)

The First Amendment's prohibition against governmental establishment of religion was written on the assumption that state aid to religion and religious schools generates discord, disharmony, hatred, and strife among our people, and that any government that supplies such aids is to that extent a tyranny.

Justice John Marshall Harlan,
concurring opinion, 392 U.S. 254.

Lemon v. *Kurtzman* (1971)

Ordinarily political debate and division, however vigorous or even partisan, are normal and healthy manifestations of our democratic system of government, but political division along religious lines was one of the principal evils against which the First Amendment was intended to protect. The potential divisiveness of such conflict is a threat to the normal political process.

> Chief Justice Warren E. Burger
> for the majority, 403 U.S. 622.

Under our system the choice has been made that government is to be entirely excluded from the area of religious instruction and churches excluded from the affairs of government.

> Ibid. at 625.

[W]hen a sectarian institution accepts state financial aid it becomes obligated under the Equal Protection Clause of the Fourteenth Amendment not to discriminate in admissions policies and faculty selection.

> Justice William J. Brennan,
> concurring opinion, ibid. at 652.

Grand Rapids School District v. *Ball* (1985)

Providing for the education of schoolchildren is surely a praiseworthy purpose. But our cases have consistently recognized that even such a praiseworthy, secular purpose cannot validate government aid to parochial schools when the aid has the effect of promoting a single religion or religion generally or when the aid unduly entangles the government in matters religious. For just as religion throughout history has provided spiritual comfort, guidance, and inspiration to many, it can also serve powerfully to divide societies and to exclude those whose beliefs are not in accord with particular religions or sects that have from time to time achieved dominance. The solution to this problem adopted by the Framers and consistently recognized by this Court is jealously to guard the right of every individual to worship according to the dictates of conscience while requiring the government to maintain a course of neutrality among religions, and between religion and non-religion.

Justice William J. Brennan
for the majority, 473 US 373.

Our cases have recognized that the Establishment Clause guards against more than direct, state-funded efforts to indoctrinate youngsters in specific religious beliefs. Government promotes religion as effectively when it fosters a close identification of its powers and responsibilities with those of any—or all—religious denominations as when it attempts to inculcate specific religious doctrines. If this identification conveys a message of government endorsement or disapproval of religion, a core purpose of the Establishment Clause is violated.

Ibid.

Appendix D

Suggestions for Further Reading

There are any number of good books on church-state relationships and the history of religious freedom in the United States. The following list includes some of the best. Asterisks indicate books available from Americans for Religious Liberty, P.O. Box 6656, Silver Spring, Maryland 20916.

Alley, Robert S., Jr. *The Supreme Court on Church and State.* New York: Oxford University Press, 1988. A thorough examination of the important rulings handed down by the nation's highest court and chief arbitrator of church-state disputes, with texts of the opinions.

Alley, Robert S., Jr., ed. *James Madison on Religious Liberty.* Amherst, N.Y.: Prometheus Books, 1985. A selection of Madison's key writings on religious liberty, plus twenty essays by distinguished scholars.

Brant, Irving. *The Bill of Rights: Its Origin and Meaning.* Indianapolis: Bobbs-Merrill, 1965. Authoritative history of the Bill of Rights. Contains a useful section on the development of the Fourteenth Amendment.

Butts, R. Freeman. *The American Tradition in Religion and Education.* Boston: Beacon Press, 1950. An overview of the role of religion in American education and a defense of religiously neutral public schools.

The Carnegie Foundation for the Advancement of Teaching. *School Choice.* Princeton, N.J., 1992. A thorough survey of choice plans for both public and nonpublic schools.

Curry, Thomas. J. *The First Freedoms: Church and State in America to the Passage of the First Amendment.* New York: Oxford University Press, 1986. An excellent history of the culture which produced the First Amendment.

Davis, Derek. *Original Intent: Chief Justice Rehnquist and the Course of American Church/State Relations.* Amherst, N.Y.: Prometheus Books, 1992. A summary of constitutional jurisprudence relating to the First Amendment.

Doerr, Edd. *Catholic Schools: The Facts.* Silver Spring, Md.: Americans for Religious Liberty, 1993. A comprehensive study of Catholic schools in the U.S., based on Catholic Church sources of information.*

Doerr, Edd, and Albert J. Menendez. *Church Schools and Public Money: The Politics of Parochiaid.* Amherst, N.Y.: Prometheus Books, 1991. A history of the politics of tax aid for nonpublic schools and the legal battles surrounding the issue at the federal and state levels.*

———. *Religious Liberty and State Constitutions.* Amherst, N.Y.: Prometheus Books, 1993. A compilation of all the religious liberty and church-state provisions of the fifty state constitutions.*

Menendez, Albert J. *Visions of Reality: What Fundamentalist Schools Teach.* Amherst, N.Y.: Prometheus Books, 1993. A critical study of the principal secular-subject textbooks used in fundamentalist private schools.*

Miller, Robert T., and Ronald B. Flowers. *Toward Benevolent Neutrality: Church, State and the Supreme Court*. Waco, Tex.: Markham Press Fund of Baylor University Press, 1992. A monumental collection of all of the major U.S. Supreme Court decisions on church and state since 1872. An essential reference.

Must, Art., Jr., ed. *Why We Still Need Public Schools*. Amherst, N.Y.: Prometheus Books, 1992. A collection of 23 illuminating essays on the importance of separation of church and state and public education.*

Peterson, Merrill D., and Robert C. Vaughn, eds. *The Virginia Statute for Religious Freedom*. New York: Cambridge University Press, 1988. A superior collection of essays probing the political culture which produced the Jeffersonian ideals of religious liberty and freedom of conscience for all citizens.

Pfeffer, Leo. *Church, State and Freedom*. Boston: Beacon Press, 1967. A thorough history of church-state relationships.

Smith, Kevin B., and Kenneth J. Meier. *The Case Against School Choice*. Armonk, N.Y.: M. E. Sharpe, 1995. Two political scientists show that school choice advocates have exaggerated public school problems and misidentified their causes. They show that the promises of school choice, public and/or private, are based on unfounded assumptions that are not borne out in practice.

Swomley, John M. *Religious Liberty and the Secular State*. Amherst, N.Y.: Prometheus Books, 1987. A summary of the foundations of religious freedom in America and an eloquent defense of the concept of secularity.*